**PUFFIN BOOKS**

*Editor: Kaye Webb*

## KNIGHTS OF GOD

Here, in a beautifully told mixture of history and legend, are the stories of some of Ireland's greatest saints, told by one of Ireland's best storytellers.

You can learn of the slavery of St Patrick, the patron saint of Ireland, of his adventurous escape, and his return to convert the Irish; of St Brendan and his strange voyages to magical, mysterious islands; of St Brigid and St Kevin and their wonderful friendships with animals, and of Lawrence O'Toole, the last in the great procession of Irish saints, who fought so hard to save Ireland from invasion by the Norman English.

*Cover design by Victor Ambrus*

# PATRICIA LYNCH

# KNIGHTS OF GOD

## TALES AND LEGENDS OF THE IRISH SAINTS

*Illustrated by*
*Victor Ambrus*

PENGUIN BOOKS

*in association with The Bodley Head*

Penguin Books Ltd, Harmondsworth, Middlesex, England
Penguin Books Australia Ltd, Ringwood, Victoria, Australia

—

First published 1945
This edition first published by The Bodley Head 1967
Published in Puffin Books 1971

—

—

Made and printed in Great Britain by
Cox & Wyman Ltd,
London, Reading and Fakenham
Set in Intertype Baskerville

To S.E.
who first told me of Saint Brendan
and his voyages

# CONTENTS

♣

# CONTENTS

# DATES OF SAINTS

❧

| | | |
|---|---|---|
| CIARAN | *born* A.D. | 385 |
| PATRICK | | 387 |
| ENDA | | 450 |
| BRIGID | | 453 |
| BRENDAN | | 484 |
| COLUMCILLE | | 487 |
| KEVIN | | 618 |
| LAWRENCE O'TOOLE | | 1123 |

# I

# SAINT CIARAN, THE FIRST
# OF THEM ALL

## Ciaran

Down the five roads of Erin:
By rath and bog they passed:
Ciaran of Clear was the first,
But who shall be the last?

# SAINT CIARAN

♣

## *The Lonely Harbour*

CIARAN lived on Clear Island, in a stone hut, above the harbour. From the doorway he could see the mainland at the other side of Roaring Water and watch the ships coming up from the south to Bantry Bay, or on to the great harbour where Cork now stands.

His father had taught him to tell where they came from by their sails, or the way the rowers held the oars and the build of the ship.

Ciaran was always wishing for a great ship to sail into their harbour, but even fishing boats, or the small coasting traders, never came there.

He longed to ask the sailors about the strange places and people they saw, their fights and adventures, but when his father, Bres, lifted their currach out from behind the great rock and rowed the boy and his mother Aideen over to the fairs or markets, Ciaran was too shy to talk to anyone.

Bres made the best oars along that coast. After a storm he walked slowly along the beach, searching for pieces of wood or trees. And Ciaran went with him.

Sometimes they were lucky, and came home, dragging their treasures over the rocks. Then Bres brought out his axe and smoothing stones, chopping and scraping until he had made something like an oar. The rest of the work he finished at night by the fire, or in stormy weather, when he couldn't go fishing or searching for wood. He scraped the flat blade, while Ciaran worked at the narrow end, and they raced to see who would finish first.

Aideen was famous for a wonderful dye she made.

Other women could knit better, but their colours seemed faded beside her brilliant blue scarves and tunics.

One winter day Bres was polishing an oar he had made from a piece of oak wood which had drifted into the harbour. The fire of shavings had burned out and the room was cold. Aideen knitted away at a long scarf, but the torch fixed on the wall above her head was smoky and gave little light, so she sat idle, rocking backwards and forwards on her low stool.

'Three days of storm,' grumbled Bres. 'What's to become of us? No fish! Nearly all the wood burned! The last bit of bread eaten and I'm hungry again!'

'There's a pot of grand soup,' Aideen told him.

'Soup!' exclaimed Bres, scornfully. 'Can a man live on soup? And will you listen to that wind?'

The thick walls shut out the storm. The roof was sound, and a great square piece of leather, thick as a board, hung over the doorway. It was fastened at one side with wooden bolts hammered into the wall, and a bar of wood thrust into slots held it in place, though, when the wind pressed against the leather, it forced a gap from top to bottom.

Ciaran stood with his face close to this narrow opening, a bit frightened when he saw how the waves were rising higher than the house before they crashed on the beach.

Yet the water in the harbour was still calm, protected on one side by a shelving tongue of rock which jutted into the sea, and on the other by the side of a cliff.

Beyond, Ciaran could see the waves climbing over one another, tossing and leaping up the cliff, yet never venturing into the harbour.

'Wouldn't you think a ship would be glad to anchor here?' thought the boy, though there wasn't a sign of anything but the brown waves and their foaming tops.

The wind beat a smother of foam against his face and he shivered, then cried out – 'A ship! A ship! A ship at last!'

'Come away to the fire, child,' said his mother. 'You're perished with the cold.'

She sighed, for the fire was only a handful of smouldering ash.

'Many's the time I fancied I saw ships, whole fleets of them, out there in a storm,' Bres told her. ' 'Tis the way the waves come pelting in. You'd swear there were sails upon sails, and sometimes 'tis just the sea birds flying low. I'll have to find wood for that fire!'

He stood up and stretched himself, letting the oar slide to the floor.

Ciaran was silent now. He had been sure, but the tips of the waves were like sails – torn sails.

He blinked, for there was salt mist on his eyelids.

'Father!' he cried. 'It is a ship! A big ship! One of the wine ships you told me about.'

Bres put his hand on the boy's shoulder and looked out over his head.

'Nonsense, lad! What would a ship be doing in that storm? Any captain that knows his trade would have made for harbour two days back.'

The wind gave the leather curtain such a blow that Ciaran fell back against his father.

'Aren't we grand and snug with a strong house between us and the storm?' said Aideen.

She rolled her knitting and poked it under her arm, then joined the two at the door.

'Surely that is a ship, can't you see it? Now! Where I'm pointing?' asked Aideen, whose eyes were even sharper than the boy's.

Ciaran saw it again, the tiny three-cornered patch of

white that wasn't the crest of a wave, or a white sea-bird, but a ship lost in that desert of water.

'I knew it was a ship!' he said proudly.

Bres saw it at last.

'The boy was right. And a wine ship too. But where are they making for? There's no sun to guide them. They can't see the shore and they'll be on the rocks before night comes. I pity them!'

'Can't we help?' cried Aideen.

Bres shook his head.

'What could we do? Show a torch? 'Twould be blown out the moment we stepped outside. And we with a fine, safe harbour waiting for them.'

Aideen clasped her hands and her bundle of knitting dropped on the floor. The colour gleamed in the dim light.

Bres snatched up the scarf.

'This will guide them!' he declared. 'If they can turn and not lose sail or mast, we may save them yet.'

They dared not take down the bar from the door, but squeezed out at the side. The noise of the waves on the rocks deafened them. The moment they stepped from shelter they felt the terrible power of the wind.

Bres looked anxiously to see if their boat was safe. It was a light currach of skin, stretched on a basket frame, and he had turned it upside-down in a hole among the rocks, far above high tide. The waves were thundering nearer and nearer, yet he thought it safe enough.

'I've never known such a sea in all my life!' he said. ' 'Twill sweep over the whole island if it keeps on. Hold tight to me, Ciaran!'

His voice could not be heard, yet still he talked.

'Aren't we foolish to venture out! There's no ship built that could live through such a storm. What can we do? They're in the power of the Sea God!'

'The look-out!' cried Aideen. 'Up the rock!'

She pointed to where steps were cut in the side of the cliff halfway up to a tiny platform which was used as a look-out.

Slowly they went towards the cliff. As they came into its shelter the wind was cut off and they could walk easily.

Bres clambered up the steps and, when he reached the platform, let the blue scarf flutter to its full length. It glowed against the grey cliff like a blue flame.

Ciaran climbed after him and Aideen followed more slowly.

'That ship will never reach the harbour!' muttered Bres. 'They'll end on the rocks yonder, or be carried out to the edge of the world!'

'She's turning this way!' cried Aideen. 'They've seen the scarf!'

The little vessel lay right over, then slipped between two waves, righted herself and came on. Now they could see a man standing upright by the mast and two others clinging to the steering oar.

'Only three!' said Bres. 'Surely there are more than three sailors on a ship that size!'

'It's going away past the island! They'll be lost in the Roaring Water!' declared Aideen. 'And they so near safety!'

She closed her eyes so that she would not see the waves conquering the ship.

'That's clever!' shouted Bres. 'They're grand shipmen! They deserve to win!'

For the ship had passed on, then, swinging suddenly, was riding the waves, and now, helped by the wind, was entering the harbour.

In his hurry to welcome the ship, Ciaran lost his footing on the slippery steps and slid the rest. He was too excited to feel bruised. Scrambling to his feet, he was stumbling across the beach when his father came up with him.

The wind caught them so that they had to turn aside to breathe. Aideen struggled along and, though the spent waves were washing over the boat slip, the three reached it as the sail dropped loosely down the mast and the ship ground against the flat rock.

The tall man standing beside the mast flung the end of a rope to Bres, who made it fast around the great stone which stood up out of sand and shingle at the head of the harbour.

He rushed to the water's edge and, as the tall man leapt on shore, greeted him.

'Thank all the gods you have come ashore alive!' he cried.

Ciaran kept close to his father. He saw the tall man's left arm was in a sling, the cloak flung back from his shoulders soaked with salt water, his wet, dark hair clinging to his head like a copper helmet. In the dim light his haughty face reminded the boy of a golden eagle he had seen flying towards the north.

Two men came ashore after him, staggering with weariness.

'Are there only three of you to sail that ship?' asked Bres.

'There were six,' said the captain. 'Two went ashore in Gaul and would come no further. They feared these strange seas. One went overboard in the storm. I tried to save him, but this arm was not strong enough. Maxen and Kyot have been with me for years. Thank God they're safe! And we must thank you. That bright blue scarf was a signal light above the waves! Without it we should never have dreamed of making for this harbour. We should never have seen it!'

As he talked, Bres and Aideen, one on each side of the captain, led him towards their hut. The two sailors, helping one another, stumbled slowly up the beach. Ciaran kept beside his mother and listened to every word.

They had almost reached the hut when the captain stopped and spoke to the sailors. At once they turned back.

'Our ship carries wine,' he explained. 'I have sent them for some.'

'Can I go too?' asked Ciaran breathlessly. 'I've never been on a ship that size.'

The captain nodded with a smile for his eagerness.

'Don't stay long!' Aideen called after the boy.

Now that the ship was safe the wind was falling. Though the waves were as strong as ever, less spray was blown in and Ciaran could run fast enough to reach the men before they were on the ship.

'The captain said I could come!' he told them.

They were friendly, though they could not understand him. Nor could he understand them when they spoke. As they climbed on board the boy began to wish he had gone straight to the hut, for he longed to listen to the captain.

The sun was setting and, though it had been hidden by clouds all day, brilliant beams shot across the stormy sky so that Ciaran could see all over the ship.

The boat was half-decked, and most of the covered space was taken up with jars and skins of wine so carefully lashed that not one was broken or torn in spite of the storm. The hold was ankle deep in water, from the waves which had dashed on board, and boxes stood up out of it. Parcels, wrapped and tied so that Ciaran could not guess what was in them, lay in soaking heaps.

Coiled ropes, nets for fishing, spare oars and sails, were

flung in a jumbled mass. A table fixed against the side, a bench and a heap of rugs showed Ciaran where the sailors lived. But he hadn't seen half when the two men each seized a tall, earthenware jar of wine and, taking a box between them, clambered off the boat again.

Ciaran went after them slowly. He thought of the captain and hurried.

'He can talk our language!' thought the boy. 'I can ask him anything I want!'

So he ran all the way to the hut and was there before the sailors.

## The Roman Captain

When Ciaran came into the hut his father was building up the fire. He had dragged in a log. It was still damp and smouldered, giving smoke but very little flame. Bres looked around. What could he burn? They must have a fire.

With a sigh he picked up one of the oars he had been making, broke it across his knee into four pieces and piled them in front of the log. At once they burst into a hot, steady flame. He broke the other and there was a blazing fire.

Aideen had bound the captain's arm with a clean white cloth and hung up his cloak on the wall, where it steamed in the warm air.

The two sailors put down the wine jars and the box. Maxen, the thin, wizened little man, opened a jar, while Kyot, a big, fat fellow, untied the rope which bound the box and flung back the lid.

Ciaran tried not to be curious, but Aideen and Bres stared with him. Aideen knew the soup was good yet she was vexed she had nothing else to offer these weary men.

The fat sailor lifted out a pasty, baked golden brown, and laid it on the table. Beside it he placed a basket of figs and some long rolls of white bread.

'A feast!' declared Bres, as pleased as if he had provided them all.

Aideen took down six wooden dishes. Each had cost a blue scarf and she was very proud of them. They were smooth, light and unbreakable. When she filled them with hot soup, Ciaran loved the golden colour which gleamed through.

The captain had the best seat at the table, opposite the fire. Aideen and Bres sat on each side. The sailors stretched on a bench against the wall. Ciaran had the stool.

Each sailor dipped a roll of bread in the soup and sucked it. Ciaran watched the captain, who broke his in small pieces. When they were soaked he ate them with a horn spoon he took from his belt.

While they ate they were silent. Aideen refilled the bowls until the cauldron was empty. The captain cut the pasty. The crust was thick and crisp. Inside were layers of pink meat, herbs and jelly. There were only three cups, so Maxen and Kyot had their wine in bowls. The captain brought out a tall, slender goblet.

'This is good wine!' said Bres. 'It lies on the tongue better than our mead. It isn't so sweet.'

'This wine comes from the far south,' the captain told him. 'There is sunshine in every drop.'

He raised his goblet.

'God keep you all!' he said.

'Who is your God?' asked Bres.

'I worship Christ,' said the captain. 'Here is his sign.'

He held out a gleaming cross which hung from a gold chain he wore about his neck. The three islanders leaned forward and Aideen touched the cross with one finger.

'You are a Christian?' she asked. 'I have heard of them. Are the sailors Christians too?'

'I am indeed a Christian!' replied the captain. 'My comrades here, though good fellows, are nothing better than heathens. They need more teaching than I can give. Where I come from there lives the leader of the Christians, and all through the city great churches are being built right beside the temples of the old pagan gods!'

'What city is that?' asked Bres.

'Rome, the Eternal!' replied the captain proudly. 'The most wonderful city in the world. The Romans are great soldiers. They make fine roads wherever they go. But the grandest thing they ever did was to build Rome. I am a Roman!'

His eyes flashed. His cheeks reddened.

Ciaran had squeezed up beside his mother. She put her arm around him and the boy leaned back against her as he listened to the captain.

'Can't we go to Rome?' he cried. 'Tomorrow when the wind goes down and the sea is smooth? Can't we get out the boat and row ourselves to Rome?'

Bres laughed. Aideen stroked her son's hair.

' 'Tis a long way,' she told him. 'The captain has a big ship, not a currach like ours!'

'If you want it enough, you'll go to Rome, that's sure!' declared the captain. 'God grant you will and that you'll become a Christian! I'll be looking forward to our meeting in Rome!'

He pushed over the basket.

'Eat figs, lad! There are plenty!'

Bres wanted to know where the captain had been and

what the people were like in strange countries, what clothes they wore, the food they ate, how they made a living. Aideen wanted to know about the Christians.

Maxen and Kyot, their legs stretched out, their arms folded, slept soundly. The thin little man was settled against the fat man's shoulder.

The log had caught fire and the smoke rose up through a slanting hole between wall and roof. The flickering flames, shot with green from the salt in the wood, gleamed on the golden cross as the captain bent forward, talking.

It was the last thing Ciaran saw before his eyes closed.

### A Busy Life

The moment Ciaran awoke he remembered the captain.

'I wonder would he let me sail with him? I'll ask!' he decided and jumped up.

The leather curtain had been taken away from the door and the morning light streamed in. Outside, on the rocks, his father was mending a tear in the hide cover of the boat. Aideen sat near him knitting a long cap.

Ciaran ran out. The wine ship was gone and with it the captain and his two sailors. The harbour was lonely once more!

Ciaran was always watching out for ships now, hoping the Roman captain would return. But before the winter Bres and Aideen packed everything they had in the currach, and the three of them crossed Roaring Water for the last time.

They had land now and a cow, and lived in a wooden

house beside a stream, too narrow for ships. When they went to fairs they drove in a cart and their life was much easier and pleasanter than when they lived on the island.

Only Ciaran missed the sea. Suppose the captain came back to the harbour and found them gone?

Ciaran learned to make the blue dye, to plant, to reap crops and grind the corn. He was able to buy and sell at markets, to use a spear and axe. Still he made no friends of his own age.

He was never lonely. On the island he had tamed sea-gulls, now he discovered all kinds of birds living in trees and bushes, and even in holes in the ground.

He was gathering sticks for the fire when he saw a finch sitting on her nest, so near he could have touched her. Suddenly a shadow flashed down – a blue-grey shadow with touches of red and orange – the shadow of the spar-rowhawk!

Ciaran saw the short, curved beak as the hawk pounced, caught the terrified finch from the nest and shot upwards.

'Oh!' cried Ciaran in horror. 'Let her go! Let the finch go!'

To his amazement the hawk stopped just above the trees, hovered, and let the finch drop. Then away it sped, though Ciaran didn't trouble to look.

The finch crouched on the ground unharmed, still too frightened to move.

'Rise up and get back to your nest!' said Ciaran. 'You know you're not hurt a bit!'

For the second time that morning a bird obeyed him. The finch gave a leap, spread her tiny wings and fluttered up to the nest. She looked at Ciaran with her round bright eyes, and Ciaran went on gathering sticks.

His life was so busy that he was a grown man before he had a chance to carry out his early dream – to go to Rome. But he learned Latin, the language of the Romans, for that would help him when he set out on his travels.

Ciaran had never forgotten the Roman captain. He recalled his words – 'I'll be looking forward to our meeting in Rome!'

Again he stepped on board a wine ship. He spoke to the captain of Rome, the Christians and their churches. But the man had no interest in anything but buying wine cheap and selling it dear. He was a bad sailor and punished the men for his own mistakes.

The paint was worn, the sail patched, the rigging a mass of knots. Another ship passed them and Ciaran envied the men who looked out over the high sides. A swift, well-kept boat! He waved but there was no answer.

'Only a fool greets strangers!' growled Captain Marius. 'Would you welcome pirates?'

'Pity I didn't choose a ship more carefully!' thought Ciaran. 'Only a fool boards a strange ship in a mist!'

He laughed. In spite of the uncared-for ship, the disagreeable captain and the sullen sailors, Ciaran was happy. He was never tired of watching the waves, the seabirds, even the seaweed drifting on the water.

For weeks they saw no land. During the day Marius steered by the sun. At night – he knew so little of the stars – they drifted.

Ciaran imagined how different this voyage would be if his Roman captain were in command. He could not talk to the sailors, for they did not speak the same language. Sometimes Ciaran was sorry he understood the captain, who growled and complained from the beginning to the end of the voyage.

They passed through the narrow channel which lies between the Pillars of Hercules and entered the Middle Sea. The water was blue as if it had been mixed with Aideen's blue dye, and Ciaran was homesick when he saw it.

They sailed along the sandy coast of North Africa and, in the distance, far beyond a savage desert, Ciaran saw mountains rising so high they reached above the clouds.

'The Mountains of Atlas. Underneath them stands a giant who carries the world on his shoulders,' Captain Marius told him. 'If ye climbed the highest, and the moon was at the full, ye could step right on to it! There's wild beasts and wilder savages on those mountains, but they're the highest in the world! Would I put ye ashore?' he asked with a grin.

'I'll see Rome first!' replied Ciaran.

He was sorry when the Mountains of Atlas passed out of sight.

The captain could not tell him when they would reach Rome.

'Best go in with other ships,' he said. 'There's pirates waiting for solitary ships, and I'm no pilot.'

They sailed within sight of land. A great burning mountain sent a shower of hot ashes across the deck and the captain gave orders to row further out.

'That's Vesuvius!' he said. 'Sometimes it only smokes. 'Tis in a bad temper now. I've seen great rivers of melted stone pouring down it!'

'Yet I can see houses, whole villages on the slopes!' cried Ciaran. 'What brave people they must be to live in such danger!'

'Fools!' declared Marius. 'Over yonder they say two great cities were buried under the flaming ashes. Long ago, that was! Herculaneum and Pompeii, they called

27

them. Some have dug there and found treasure. More found corpses!'

Ciaran determined to watch all night, so that he would not miss one moment of Rome. The captain delayed so long the young man fell asleep. They sailed up the Tiber while he slept and he did not awake until shouts of 'Roma! Roma!' from men in small boats, coming from the shore, told him he had reached the Eternal City.

### Ciaran Enters Rome

'There's Rome!' said Marius. 'Our voyage ends here.'

Ciaran looked at the swirling, yellow river. Then at the lights which rose beyond the city walls.

'I'll go ashore at dawn,' he said. He could not believe he had reached Rome.

'Ye'll go ashore tonight,' the captain told him. 'I'm going and I'll leave no stranger on board my ship.'

'Then I'll go with you!' declared Ciaran.

Marius laughed. He was friendlier now. He hailed one of the small boats and, with Ciaran, clambered over the side.

A line of wooden huts stretched along the bank into the darkness. Only one, the largest, showed a light, and Marius tramped through the mud towards it.

He pushed at the door which swung inward and Ciaran saw a room so crowded that, though long tables ran from end to end, there was no vacant space. Men leaned against the walls eating and drinking, as they stood between others who sat on the floor, their heads on their knees, sleeping.

Several shouted, 'Ho, Marius! What luck?' and they raised their drinking mugs.

The captain shouted back, but the uproar was so great that no one could tell what he said. Groups sang in chorus and men, seated side by side, had to shout in one another's ears.

'This is no place for a man that needs food and rest!' grumbled Marius, glaring around him.

A dark woman, carrying a jar of wine, went along the tables, filling empty mugs. When she saw Marius she beckoned him through a doorway into a small, wooden shed, built against the larger hut. An old man, with long white hair, sat at a table eating bread and olives. Marius sat on the bench opposite and pulled Ciaran down beside him.

The woman closed the door, shutting out the noise.

'Well, Pietro!' said the captain. 'I'm back!'

He stretched his legs out under the table and flung his arms above his head.

The old man smiled and bit at an olive.

'Was the sea kind to you, Marius?' he asked.

The captain shook his head.

'Neptune is the most unfriendly of the gods!' he declared. 'If I had a wine shop on dry land I'd be the happiest man alive. But here's a stranger,' he went on. 'He comes from an island in the far ocean, the land of the Scots, Erin they call it. I have a good cargo on board.'

The old man stopped eating.

'What do you seek in Rome?' he asked Ciaran.

'When I was a boy I met a Roman, a Christian. I've never forgotten him. I wanted to see his city and, if I could, become a Christian too. I have never known any man like him.'

'Where's the sense in coming to Rome to find a Roman?' demanded Captain Marius. 'Listen to the noise in the long room. Every man speaks a different language.

There are Syrians, Jews, labourers from Sicily and Africa, marble cutters from the south. There are a few bargemen who were born along the Tiber – but Romans! You, Pietro, and the woman are the only Romans here!'

'It is right that all nations should meet in Rome!' said Pietro. 'Rome is the centre of the world. But this is not the city. Tomorrow I will show your friend Rome. There he will become a Christian.'

'Are there no Christians in your own country?' asked Marius. 'A man who is not a shipman, yet ventures on the sea, is a fool!'

Pietro asked no questions, but he, too, looked at Ciaran curiously.

'I did hear of Christians in my own country but not in the part I come from,' said the young man. 'The only Christian I met was a Roman captain whose ship took refuge in our harbour. He was with us for one night only; but he told me of Rome. He said it was the most wonderful city in the world. Perhaps I shall find him here.'

Marius flung back his head and laughed.

'He seeks a captain he saw once years ago, and he seeks him in Rome. Why, man! There are more people in Rome than in the whole of your country!'

'And yet,' Pietro told him, 'I have heard it said that if a man should wait long enough at the Forum, he would see everyone he knew.'

Marius grinned.

'Our friend here is young. He can afford to spend a few years waiting for his Roman on the Forum.'

The woman put a dish of stewed goat flesh on the table, two mugs and a jar of wine. Ciaran was too excited to eat. He wanted to see Rome.

Marius finished the stew, emptied the jar of wine and set his elbows on the table, singing to himself.

'Sleep, stranger,' said Pietro, pointing to a heap of straw in the corner.

Ciaran used his bundle for a pillow. He had twelve scarves wrapped in it and they made a soft resting place for his head.

'Where will I sell them?' he wondered. 'The bigger the price the longer I can stay in Rome.'

He closed his eyes. For a long time he listened to the captain's song. He saw the Roman captain striding up from the harbour and tried to run to him. He stumbled on the rocks and his feet sank into the sand. A hand seized his shoulder. He started up.

Old Pietro had roused him. Marius was stretched on the floor, his head pillowed on his arm.

'I go abroad early,' said the old man. 'I am a stone-cutter and must catch all the hours of daylight. But first I will go with you.'

They ate a breakfast of dry bread and olives. The bread was dark and sweet. Ciaran liked it better than any bread he had eaten before, though he could not eat the sour olives. Pietro put them in his pocket to nibble as he walked along.

Ciaran took out one of his scarves.

'I have twelve,' he told the old man. 'I must sell them, for I have no money.'

Pietro picked up the scarf and examined it. Ciaran watched him anxiously.

'Beautiful!' exclaimed the old man, feeling the fine, silky wool. 'A skilled craftswoman made this. And the colour! I have never seen such a blue! It should hang behind the Madonna's statue in Saint Peter's.'

'Then I will be able to sell them!' cried Ciaran. 'Captain Marius brought me here for one.'

'We must go to the Forum,' said the old man. 'There I

31

will find generous buyers for your scarves. Yet first to Saint Peter's. You have waited so long, you must become a Christian before anything else!'

They went out through the long room where sleepers were stretched on the earthen floor, so that the two men had to step over them.

A heavy mist lay on the marshes, reaching back on each side of the river. Masts rose up through the mist, but the ships were hidden.

'A mist that breeds fevers. Do not breathe it!' warned Pietro, covering his mouth with a corner of the long, black cloak he wore.

Barges, loaded with blocks of yellow-grey stone, were moored by the bank. Dark-skinned labourers lifted the blocks on to low carts drawn by oxen and, as these moved slowly away towards the city gates, Ciaran gazed after them.

He touched Pietro's arm.

'So many cities!' he cried. 'Are they all Rome?'

Pietro was pleased. He was very proud of his native city.

'Rome of the Seven Hills!' he said. 'Remember it is an old city. It is over four hundred years since Christ was born and Romulus built the first wall more than seven hundred years before that. And all the time Romans have been building Rome!'

Ciaran stared at the great wall which began at the Tiber, bounded a hill crowned with temples and triumphal arches, crossed a valley and curved by the edge of another hill of stone and marble buildings, out of sight.

Pietro led him through a gateway and they began to climb the nearest hill.

Across the valley a great aqueduct, bringing water to the city, marched from the hills where dark, massive cypresses looked black against the rich blue sky. The river was still hidden in mist but the blazing sun was climbing over the hills. Ciaran, who had shivered as they came from the inn, now opened his tunic and wiped his hot face.

Pietro showed him the seven hills and Ciaran repeated the names after him until he knew them all – the Capitoline, Palatine, Aventine, Caelian, Virminal, Esquiline and Quirinal.

'They sound like music,' thought the young man.

But it seemed to him as if all the people around talked as if they were singing.

They came into the streets, paved with blocks of lava from the slopes of Mount Vesuvius. The pavements were crowded. Ciaran had never heard such noise, or seen such bright clothes. He had never dreamed there were so many people in the world.

Pietro loved Rome. He knew the history of every building in the city, every statue and even the ruins. But they were bound for the Church of Saint Peter's.

Following a line of market carts, piled with baskets of grapes and figs, along a narrow street they came into a square. A flight of wide stone steps led up to a great church with bronze doors. On the steps sat women selling flowers, mulberries and pomegranates. In front, a fountain rose into the hot air and Ciaran cried out in wonder, for it was the first he had seen and he could not understand where the fine spray came from and what happened when it spattered back into the marble basin. Bells clashed from every tower and steeple so that the air rocked.

The doors of the church were continually swinging, for people were going in and out all the time.

'The Emperor Nero's Circus was here in the old days,' said Pietro. 'He was the one that persecuted the Christians

and had Saint Peter crucified. Now on the ruins of his
Circus is the Church of Saint Peter.'

He stopped talking as they climbed the steps and hurried after a monk who was entering the church.

'Here is a foreigner who would be a Christian,' panted
the old man.

The monk turned, his dark face smiling in welcome.

Day after day Ciaran came to Saint Peter's and to the
courts behind it where the students gathered. He had so
much to learn that often he stumbled out into the streets
after the gates were closed, for he not only wanted to
become a Christian, but he was determined to preach
Christianity in his own country.

Pietro found him a lodging with other Christians who
lived in an old house near the Forum, where the great
processions started. The house was built over the cata-
combs, and one day Pietro took him down into the dark
galleries. By the flickering light of candles Ciaran saw the
altars where the early Christians worshipped, the cells
where they lived and the tombs where they were
buried.

Dreaming of ancient times Ciaran wandered down the
Appian Way, the road of tombs, and listened to the old
man telling of the Goths and Vandals.

'They besieged Rome again and again,' he said. 'You
can still see the marks of their burnings. They were barbarians and lived to kill and destroy. When they came
raging across the Campagna all thought it was the end of
Rome. They did not understand that Rome is eternal and
cannot be destroyed!'

They came back by the Coliseum, that great round
building, so huge, Ciaran could not believe it had been
built by men.

He stood in the arena and gazed up at the rows and

rows of seats towering above him. There had sat the Emperor and there the Vestal Virgins.

'Here gladiators fought with one another,' Pietro told him, 'and with savage animals. Here Christian men, women and children were killed for believing in Christ, and thousands watched them die.'

As Ciaran went through Rome he would see a tall figure, head flung back, striding through the crowd.

'There's the Roman captain!' he would cry and, hurrying after, discover a stranger.

### Ciaran Meets Patrick

Ciaran's scarves were sold, the money spent. His purse was empty.

'There's always work in Rome,' Pietro told him. 'No need to be hungry here.'

'I must go back!' said Ciaran.

Still he stayed. He copied manuscripts and earned all he needed. In time he became a priest and learned all he could so that he might teach his own people. He read until he loved books and always carried one in his hand.

At last he said good-bye to Pietro. He did not say good-bye to Rome until he looked back from the hills outside the city. He stood in the shadow of a cypress, while carts carrying logs of wood passed him. The drivers lounged half-asleep, the plodding oxen scattered dust at every step and the bells round their necks tinkled. Ciaran longed to go with them, yet he longed still more for his own country.

Church bells were ringing as he trudged southwards, for he had determined to return another way.

Ciaran came one evening to a little walled town

above the sea. The gates were closing as he entered, and women were filling jars with water at a fountain in the square.

He stopped to drink and wash the dust from his face and hands. Opposite the fountain was a low, stone church and, as he walked towards it, a tall man wearing a long cloak thrown back at the shoulders, came out. Ciaran had grown used to the Roman face, dark, with strong nose and chin, and steady eyes. But there was something more familiar about this man.

The only disappointment Ciaran had known since he sailed up the Tiber vanished. Forgetting in his haste the bundle and staff he had laid down, he went straight across the square.

A good-natured man ran after him.

'Your package and your stick, friend!' he called.

The crowd was dense, but seeing Ciaran was a stranger people made way for him, and Ciaran came up with the man in the cloak as he turned into a side street.

'Roman captain!' he cried. 'I feared I would never see you again. Your wish for me has come true. I have been to Rome. I am a Christian and a priest!'

The tall man listened with a puzzled smile.

'Your news makes me very happy. But are you sure I am your Roman captain?'

Ciaran looked earnestly into his face.

'It is years ago,' he said slowly. 'I was only a child, but I have always remembered you. I looked for you in Rome. Only such numbers of people are there.'

'What was your captain's name?' asked the tall man.

Ciaran shook his head.

'I do not know!'

And he told the story of the storm.

'I wish you could find your friend,' said the other. 'My

name is Patrick, and God must have willed us to meet, for I, too, come from Erin. I was a slave there, up in the north. It is my ambition to go back and preach the religion of Christ.'

'Take me with you!' pleaded Ciaran.

'You are on your way. Tomorrow a ship sails for the western seas. You will journey on that ship. I am not ready yet. But I will come, Ciaran, I promise!'

'When will you come?' asked Ciaran.

'I cannot say. When you reach your country seek for the well at Fuaran. There build an oratory and I will come.'

'I've never heard of the place!' declared Ciaran. 'How shall I find it?'

Patrick took a bell from under his cloak and put it into Ciaran's hands.

'This bell will guide you. It will not make a sound before you come to the well at Fuaran. Then it will ring with a clear note. Be silent as the bell. Do not speak to anyone until the bell rings. Remember – it may be a long time – but I will come!'

### The Journey Home

The ship was at sea before the captain discovered a stranger among the rowers.

'Who gave you leave to come aboard?' he shouted.

Ciaran looked up, placed his finger to his lips and rowed steadily, keeping exact time with the others.

'He will not speak, master. He must be under a vow of silence,' exclaimed one of the men.

The captain frowned. He lacked one man and the silent stranger rowed well.

'He shall have his food, nothing more,' he decided. 'I did not engage him.'

So Ciaran rowed his way to Gaul.

There, still keeping silence, he found a ship setting out for the south of Britain. Ciaran helped with the sail, cooked food and listened to the stories the men told of their homes and their wanderings.

When they reached port the men were so loaded with clothes and food they had bought from the little rowing-boats swarming to meet the bigger vessels that they staggered up the rocky shore. Outside an inn for sailors, they stood in a group and stared at Ciaran. In spite of his silence he had been the friendliest in the crew and they were all sorry to part with him.

He gazed at the harbour, wondering which of the boats moored there would be sailing for Erin.

The man who had rowed in front of Ciaran gave him a slap on the shoulder and thrust a pair of new sandals into his hands.

'May the gods be good to you, for you're a good ship-mate though you don't talk,' he chuckled. 'Hi, lads! Shall our silent friend come ashore like a beggar?'

The seamen crowded round Ciaran laughing and pushing. A warm cloak was flung over his shoulders, a sack of cakes laid at his feet, and two silver pieces pressed into his hand.

Shouting, the men tramped through the doorway of the inn and Ciaran was left alone by the sea wall.

Not quite alone. A heap of rags lay near him on the stones. This stirred and an old, old woman stood up shivering. She was thin and bent. Her grey hair straggled over her face and she peered through it at Ciaran.

He was smiling at the sailors' generosity as he pulled off his old broken sandals and flung them away.

Before they fell the old woman snatched and caught them. Ciaran stepped over and knelt before her. He slipped the new sandals on her bony feet, cut and bruised by the sharp stones.

Ciaran wrapped the cloak over her rags, took one cake and placed the full sack on the stones where she sat. Then he gave her one of the silver pieces and a silent blessing.

'What do I want with money, or the burden of clothes and food?' he thought, pulling on the old sandals and striding off in search of a boat.

The old woman sat hugging herself.

'That lad must be one of those Christians I've heard tell of,' she muttered, her face growing even more wrinkled with happiness. 'Food and warmth and kindness from a stranger – what more could an old beggar woman ask?'

The last part of Ciaran's journey was the hardest. Some ship-masters dreaded pirates, others would not venture across to the Unknown Land, as they called Ireland. They told Ciaran that strange monsters and men without fear lived there.

'Must I build a boat before I can reach my own country?' he thought.

He was feeling desolate, one moment wishing he had never gone travelling, the next that he had stayed in Rome.

'How easy to go away; how hard to return,' Ciaran reflected.

He was wandering along a strip of rock where a man and woman were patching a leaky fishing boat. At once he went to help them. Ciaran worked twice as fast as the two together. When the work was finished, without a word of thanks they pushed the boat down to the water and scrambled in. Ciaran followed.

The man let a net out over the side. It was broken and

if fish came in they could as easily go out. Ciaran drew it back and rewove the broken strands. While he worked wind and tide swept the boat out to sea, beyond sight of land.

Ciaran was so busy he did not notice. His companions sat watching. When the net was mended Ciaran looked up and discovered they were drifting into shore. They had crossed the sea and he had reached his own country.

Ciaran folded the net and laid it in the bottom of the boat. Holding his bundle he leaped ashore.

The fisher people didn't bother to look after him. They were letting out their net.

'God grant you go safely home!' thought Ciaran.

As he walked up from the sea Ciaran slipped on the thick seaweed. The bell, which he had fastened to his belt, struck a rock, but there wasn't a sound from it.

'Why would there be?' he asked himself. 'There isn't a well in sight.'


### The Bell Rings

Ciaran found a road and followed it. Before evening he came to a well. The water was cold and clear, with a sparkle in it. He drank and washed himself, but there was never a sound from the bell.

The road kept near the coast. Sometimes it was a fine highway where two chariots could pass. Then it would grow rough and narrow so that only those who walked could use it.

Ciaran met other roads but did not look at them.

'Time enough to go exploring when the bell rings,' he thought.

When he had been among foreigners, unless they knew

Latin, he could not speak with them. Now he was among those who spoke his own language and it was hard to keep silent. People on their way to fairs walked beside him, talking of the price of grain and mead and of the long distances on bad roads. Drivers, liking the look of him, slowed up to offer a lift. Women tending fires, or washing clothes in a stream, called out, wishing Ciaran a safe journey, and he could only smile at them.

Ballad-singers and story-tellers were the best companions. They didn't want him to talk, only to listen, and Ciaran was a good listener.

When the road went round a bay he was glad to cross in a boat. If it went inland along the bank of a river to a bridge, he watched out for a ford.

'Isn't the straight way the best when a man is in a hurry?' he asked himself.

The road went through a thick wood and night was coming on. Ciaran walked in darkness yet he could see sunlight beyond the trees. He went slowly, wondering where he could find shelter.

'I might climb a tree,' he thought. 'No! I wouldn't care for that. What about seeking for a hollow trunk? I can hear rain falling on the leaves.'

He couldn't make up his mind and kept walking. As he came out from the protection of the trees a sharp wind swept rain in his face and he was tempted to turn back.

The bell hanging to his belt gave a faint tinkle.

'No!' cried Ciaran. 'It can't be. There's no well here, only a dark wood and a rocky valley.'

The bell sounded a loud clear note and there before him, in a sandy basin with a wall of smooth stones about it, was a well of clear water gleaming in the evening light.

Beside it was a hole among the rocks and there Ciaran

lay, eating his supper, while the bell rang for company.

He heard the rain falling as he fell asleep but the morning rose fine and clear. Ciaran said his prayers, had a good drink of water, finished his bread and went into the wood to gather branches.

He had a good pile of them and was feeling tired, so he sat with his back against a giant beech to rest.

Ciaran heard a rustling in the bushes and he saw the fierce red eyes of a wild boar peering at him.

'I never saw such tusks in my life,' declared Ciaran who, since he must not talk to anyone else, talked to himself. He looked straight in front, expecting the boar to attack him, but the fierce creature only moved a little closer and gazed at him beseechingly.

'I do believe you're as lonely as I am,' said Ciaran. 'But I can't sit here talking while there's work to be done.'

He stood up slowly, determined to show no fear, and went into the wood. He broke a branch. The boar broke a larger one and dragged it out to the heap.

'Thank you, friend boar!' said Ciaran. 'If you'll bring the wood, I can start building.'

They worked together, Ciaran planting the branches in a circle and binding them at the top. He left space for a doorway and made a fireplace of stones, the boar bringing him logs for the fire.

'All I need now is something to cook,' chuckled Ciaran.

Stealing in and out among the trees came a fox, a fat goose dangling from its jaws. He set it down before Ciaran and stood there looking at him with a sly grin.

Ciaran and the fox shared the goose between them and from that day there was no need to worry about food.

Another day a badger made friends with Ciaran, and

before winter a wolf made his home in the hole which had sheltered the monk on his first night at the well.

With spring came a fallow deer, showing no dread of the wolf, for Ciaran had the power of making all living creatures friends with one another.

When Ciaran took off his sandals to dry, the fox loved playing with the thongs. He dragged at them and jumped, with the sandals jumping after him. Ciaran laughed at the fox's antics but hung his sandals high.

For days the fox had no chance of playing with the sandals. Then Ciaran, paddling in the brook in search of watercress, left them on the bank. The fox seized the thongs and dragged them into the wood. When Ciaran returned there was no sign of the sandals.

'Find Brother Fox and tell him he should not play tricks on his master,' said Ciaran to the badger.

Off went the badger, dodging in and out among the trees, sniffing the ground until he found the fox's trail. He ran swiftly and came upon the fox lying under a sunny bank chewing the sandals.

The badger gave Ciaran's message. The fox grinned and went on chewing.

The badger became angry, gave a leap, caught the fox by the ear and tried to drag him away from the sandals.

The fox would not let go. The badger dragged and tugged until he pulled fox and sandals out of the wood and back to the hut.

The other animals stood around and stared severely at the fox. Ciaran didn't punish him. He didn't even scold him. He put on his chewed sandals and told the animals how it was with people. If they respected one another, if they lived as friends, they were happy. If they played tricks, stole and tormented one another, they had no peace or happiness.

The fox was ashamed. He determined to play no more tricks and became one of Ciaran's best friends.

Ciaran preached to his animals. Presently people coming to the well for water stayed to listen.

'When Patrick comes we shall have a church and be proper Christians,' Ciaran promised them.

He found a little fish in the well and every day it came to be fed. One day a poor woman with a sick child leaned over the well to draw a jug of water. The fish leaped up and she saw its glistening back. When she went home her child was healed. After that anyone sick who caught sight of the fish was cured. All those who were strong and those who had been cured helped Ciaran to build a stone oratory, ready for the coming of Patrick.

Ciaran hung Patrick's bell over the entrance, and every time it rang he climbed the hill to watch out for Patrick.

One night he could not sleep. He lay thinking of his childhood, of the Roman captain and then of Patrick, a Roman too.

'They seem one to me now,' he thought. 'But how lonely and weary is this waiting!'

Ciaran stood up and went out of the hut. Dawn was coming over the wood. The tops of the trees were touched with gold. He could hear the crackling of dried leaves and twigs. Strangers were coming.

He climbed the hill which rose above his oratory. Now he could see to where a wide river flowed into the ocean. Long, rolling waves, flecked with foam like the white on a gull's throat, broke along the beach.

At the horizon, clouds piled against the sky.

'Are they clouds?' wondered Ciaran. Turrets, golden and rose coloured, stood beyond the waves. Towers, white or palest blue, rose from glowing roofs. Dawn came, through windows shaped like flowers and stars.

Ciaran had heard stories of Falias, Gorias, Finias, Murias – ancient magic cities of the Dananns who lived in Ireland before the days of history. They were built in a single night, each with its special treasure.

'Can this be one of those cities?'

Then seven hills rose beyond the glittering roofs and Ciaran gazed once more upon the glories of Rome, while the bell of Saint Patrick rang from the oratory.

The fox barked as Ciaran ran down. The wolf flung back his head and howled until Ciaran ordered him to be quiet. All his animal friends drew close, preparing to defend him.

A man in a white robe, carrying a long staff and followed by a procession of priests and attendants, stepped out from the wood.

'Ciaran!' he said. 'I have come at last!'

The bell rang loudly, though no one touched it and not the lightest wind was stirring.

'Patrick! I kept my word!' cried Ciaran.

'You shall be a hermit no longer!' Patrick told him. 'My work is beginning and we shall make of Ireland a Christian country rich with churches and schools. All along the five roads the chiefs and the people await us. Here, Ciaran, found your monastery, for here shall your glory and your resurrection be. And you shall be the first of the saints of Erin.'

## 2

# SAINT PATRICK,
# THE ROMAN
# SLAVE

## Patrick

They brought him as a slave across the sea –
A homesick Roman boy, lonely and sad.
Then a voice called and led him far away –
A wanderer, not a slave, yet not quite free,
Until he dreamed and knew our land his own.

He lit a fire on Slane above the Boyne
And every hill in Ireland gleamed with light.
He went to Tara – Tara of the Kings.
The pagan gods were beaten, darkness fled.

On every road we walk his feet have trod.
The dawn was in his eyes and in his mind
Brave thoughts and kind: our greatest saint
A travelling man, a slave, a shepherd boy.

# SAINT PATRICK

♣

## The Raiders

PATRICK always loved wandering. When he should
have been learning with the other boys he was at the
harbour, listening to the fishermen, envying the sailors on
the ships and climbing the high rocks to stare after them.
Once he trudged inland all the way to the great road to
see a legion marching south, on its way back to Rome.
'You'd do better to mind your books!' declared his father,
Calpornius. 'A slave would have more sense!'

Calpornius was rich and important – a Roman citizen
as well as a Christian. He had a grand villa in the town,
built of stone with black and white tiled floors. The high
rooms had padded sofas and woven silk curtains. In the
entrance stood two statues in marble and bronze, and the
whole house was heated to keep out the damp and cold.

Calpornius wanted a son he could be proud of, wise
and learned, who might go to Rome one day.

'Time enough,' said Patrick's mother. 'He's a good lad,
kind, though he is a bit wild. But he'll learn.'

The farmhouse above the river, where Patrick and the
other children spent most of their time, was a pleasant
house with an apple orchard at the back and the big cider
press in a wooden shed among the trees. At the bottom of
the meadow which ran by the house were the stables, the
barns and huts for beasts and slaves. Along the bank huddled the fishermen's hovels and the sheds where galleys
were built and goods stored when the trading ships came
in.

The sea mist was still on the river when Patrick climbed
the height above the bank. He could see across to the

49

farmhouse and the wheat fields beyond. Blue smoke from wood fires was rising above villas in clearings among the trees and on the slopes of the mountains. Slaves were coming out to work in the fields, and an ox cart lumbered along the road which led inland through the gap. A woman, washing clothes at the river, sat back on her heels, and began to sing –

> 'There's a boat on the river,
> Sailing down to the sea.
> Beyond the sea it journeys
> To Rome of the seven hills.'

Patrick knew the song and sang with her. Suddenly he stopped. A ship, a strange ship, was coming up the river.

'Now where would that be from?' he wondered, peering through the mist.

None of the regular ships was due that day. But he was always hoping that a ship travelling from a strange country, bound for unknown seas, would enter the harbour and that his father would allow him to go away on it in search of dragons and unicorns.

'There's another!' he cried, jumping up.

Perhaps his wish was coming to him!

The little settlement had been peaceful for so long that Patrick did not dream of danger. He knew there was fighting always in the north where walls had been built to keep back the barbarians. He had heard of raiders from the land across the sea who descended upon the Roman garrisons in the south and west, but in this hidden corner, so far up the great river, nothing happened from one year's end to another.

The long narrow shields hung idle on the walls of the Roman houses. Spears and battle-axes were flung care-

lessly into chests. In distant Rome there might be war with
the Goths, the savage Picts attacked the outposts on the
northern walls: all along the coasts Niall of the Nine Hostages was raiding and harrying, but here there was peace.
The men working in the fields, fishermen mending their
nets, women picking apples in the orchards or washing
clothes at the river, went on with their work, as Patrick
saw the foreign ships, with all sails set, speeding through
the mist towards them.

Now three, now four, now a whole fleet spread across
the river, then drew into the harbour below the watching
boy.

Still he was untroubled until he saw gleaming, round
bronze shields and long iron spears clutched by men who
crowded the sides of the ships. On the high prow of the
first ship stood a black-haired man, holding a curved horn
longer than Patrick himself!

'Raiders!' he cried. 'Raiders!'

As he turned to run he was seen from the ships – a tall,
thin boy in a white linen tunic with an embroidered
border, bare legs and fine, leather sandals on his feet. His
thick, short hair gleamed as he leaped from rock to rock
like a goat. There was a path, but Patrick chose the shortest way.

He was halfway down when the man with the horn
lifted it to his lips and blew. Such a terrible snarling and
growling arose that Patrick stopped in amazement.

'There must be a fearful monster on that ship!' thought
the boy. 'No! It's just that horn!'

He did not pause again until he reached the bank.

'Raiders!' he shouted. 'Raiders!'

Another blast from the war horn drowned his voice.
The women washing clothes scrambled up, and a blue
dress floated unheeded down the river. Fishermen came

stumbling out of their huts, nets trailing after them, and stared stupidly at the queerly built ships and the crowding warriors with their strange arms. Patrick raced across the road and up towards the farmhouse. He met the men who had been working in the fields and, still carrying their scythes and forks, came hurrying to discover what the uproar meant.

'Arm yourselves!' cried Patrick. 'We must fight!'

One of his father's slaves, a huge man, a spade on his shoulder, pushed the boy away.

'Who can stand against Niall of the Nine Hostages and his pirates?' he exclaimed. 'I know that war horn! Hide! Make for the woods or the mountains! Hide!'

'We are Romans! Who dare attack us?' demanded the steward, a lazy, dignified man.

But he clambered over a wall and ran towards the trees.

Since Patrick was a very small boy he had heard stories of the great fighting king, whose hostages were princes and who sailed the seas wherever there were ships to seize or towns to attack.

The paths were crowded with women carrying children, men dragging bags of money, precious statues and furniture. Patrick was pushed back against the wall. He was nearly knocked over and he was deafened by screams of fear, people shouting orders to one another and, rising over all, the terrible threat of the war horn.

'If only my father were here!' said Patrick. 'He'd know what to do.'

But Calpornius was across the mountains at his town villa.

The last ship had entered the harbour. The sails dropped down. Holding their swords and shields above their heads, the raiders leaped ashore. Britons who had snatched up swords and axes marched to meet them, but the frightened mob on the road prevented them from using their weapons and they were killed without a chance to defend themselves.

The invaders split into small groups. Some went into the houses, which they plundered, then set on fire. Others, seizing the strong men and women, and the young boys and girls, drove them down to the ships.

Patrick was caught in the crush. He kicked and struggled, but he was thrust into the water and hauled on board the first ship. He was still struggling when he was flung into the hold, already packed with captives from an earlier raid.

He could hear the shouts and cries of men fighting with scythes and forks, the crackle and roar of burning huts. Now rose the war horn calling the warriors back. They came loaded with silk hangings, rich clothes, jewels, and weapons which the Romanized Britons had forgotten how to use.

At once the ships pushed off. The strongest of the captives were put to the oars to bring the vessels out of the harbour. Bewildered by the suddenness of his misfortune, Patrick sat hugging his knees. He could not believe that his home was burning, himself a prisoner and that he might never see his mother and father again.

'What will become of us?' asked one of the prisoners, as they crouched on the bare planks.

'We shall be sold as slaves!' declared a young man. 'We are being taken to the Unknown Land. God knows what hardships we shall meet among the pagans!'

Patrick stood up, determined to jump overboard and swim to freedom. But the ships were in full sail, almost at the mouth of the river. Great waves from the sea were thundering towards them. Along the shore he could see more burning buildings, for this had been a great raid.

The lurching of the ship sent him sprawling. He huddled in a corner and presently fell asleep. He woke and slept, woke and slept, until he lost track of the hours, but, stiff and hungry, he was the first of all the captives to see the blue mountains of the Unknown Land.


## The Silent Man

In those days Ireland was called the Land of the Scots and, as Patrick stood in the slave market, he looked at strange people and listened to a strange tongue, for the speech of his people and of all throughout the Roman world was Latin, while these spoke Gaelic.

For hours the raiders had been selling their captives to the merchants. Now the raiders were feasting and the slaves waiting for new masters.

Patrick's tunic was torn and dirty. He had lost one of his sandals and he wore chains on his ankles. Yet he stood proudly, though he was weary with hunger and loneliness.

He was afraid, too, and he had never been afraid before. His happy life at the Roman settlement seemed to belong to years ago.

'They can't make me a slave!' he thought indignantly.

All around him captives were being sold. The men and women went first. Though they cost more they were less trouble than younger slaves and could work harder. Still the market was crowded, as this had been the biggest raid for years.

Patrick forgot his own troubles when he saw boys he had played with marched off to slavery. The younger ones were crying, but rubbed their tears away when they were taken over to a tent where loaves of bread were cut into slices and a yellow drink poured out from tall, earthenware jars.

'When will my turn come?' he wondered, for his mouth was parched and the smell of hot bread made him hungrier than ever.

Pushing his way slowly through the crowd came a short, broad man with sandy hair and pale blue eyes. He pursed his lips as though he were whistling, but not a sound came from them. When an acquaintance stopped him, he listened, his head on one side, nodded, shook his head, then gazed into the distance.

'If the silent one buys ye, 'twill be great luck for me,' the merchant who had bought Patrick said to him in a queer kind of Latin. 'But I'll be sorry for ye. Runner and dealer he is to Melcho, Prince in Dalaradia.'

'Why should that make you sorry?' asked Patrick.

The merchant shook his head mournfully.

'Melcho is known throughout the length and breadth of the land for a harsh, cruel tyrant. He's brave enough, and clever, yet he has no kindness and little learning. Still, I've me debts to pay, so stand straight and look as if ye could work hard.'

Patrick hated the sandy man when he saw him pull a boy to his feet, pinch his arms, feel his legs, force open the lad's mouth to look at his teeth, then with a scornful shake of the head, pass on.

Merchants crowded round him, thrusting boys forward, shouting, clutching his plain, brown tunic, but all he did was to shake his head and move steadily through the market.

At last he came to where Patrick stood alone. He stared at the young Roman and the young Roman stared back.

'How dare he treat us like cattle!' thought the boy. 'We are Romans!'

But the silent man did not touch Patrick. He nodded, turned to the merchant at his elbow and waited.

The merchant talked. Patrick couldn't understand a word, and the sandy-haired stranger stood silent until the other stopped for want of breath. Then he spoke one word.

The merchant flung up his hands in horror and began to talk again. The sandy-haired man swung round and was walking away, when the merchant caught him by the tunic.

'They're bargaining for me as if I were a horse!' muttered Patrick indignantly.

Yet he was curious about this man who refused to speak.

He still stood when the merchant, bending down, unfastened Patrick's chains and gave him a push. The other pulled out a large gold piece from the leather bag which hung from his belt, placed it in the merchant's outstretched hand, put a second and a third beside it.

'Come, Roman slave!' he said, speaking in as good Latin as ever Patrick had heard his father use. Without a glance to see if the boy followed, he strode off.

Patrick hurried to keep up, eager to hear the sandy-haired man speak again. But the crowd was so dense he had to force his way until they were on the outskirts of the slave market.

Here stalls and booths were ranged in rows, each row selling the same kind of goods. There were gleaming fish from the river, lobsters and salmon from the sea. Great brown cakes of bread, as large as cartwheels, were piled high. Small, sweet cakes and combs of honey were heaped in straw baskets. Farther on, glittering ornaments were spread out, though the finer pieces of gold, studded with gems, were secure in chests, opened only for special customers. There were silks and embroidered stuffs and rolls of purple cloth with glittering threads. Gaily-dressed women, their servants carrying baskets, walked slowly along, fingering the stuffs, admiring the ornaments, trying on gold hair nets and ear-rings, collars of beaten gold, rings set with dull purple stones, but buying the fish and bread.

Patrick had never seen such helmets and shields, made of bronze and beautifully decorated. There were spearheads too, and swords. Limping painfully, he longed for the shoes and sandals strung up on poles. The carved chessboards, with their jewelled corners, set out with chess men in gold and silver, and red and white ivory, made him see his father and mother bending thoughtfully over a drawn-out game.

The sandy-haired man was as interested as Patrick. He stopped and watched two jugglers, one tossing coloured balls into the air and keeping as many as a dozen spinning at a time, the other doing tricks with sharp, pointed knives. They halted at a circle of people gathered about a storyteller and, looking at the eager intent faces, Patrick wished he understood the story.

But he had not eaten for many hours. Since his last proper meal disaster had come upon him and his whole life was changed. Patrick's head was dizzy, he stumbled and nearly fell, only his companion put an arm around the boy's shoulders and brought him into a cool, dark tent.

'I, Flann, am a fool!' he declared. 'I should know the raiders do not waste food on captives!'

Patrick was thankful to sit on the rough form alongside the trestle table. He leaned his head in his hands and did not move until a bowl of thick, steaming soup and a hunk of bread were slapped down before him. He had a bone spoon still safe in his belt and he began to eat at once. Suddenly he laid down the spoon and gazed at the sandy-haired man who already was cleaning his bowl with a piece of bread.

'Are you a Roman, too?' he asked.

The man grinned.

'Not I! Flann, a Roman? Have sense, lad!'

'But you speak as we do!'

'I speak many tongues. I have travelled far.'

'When I saw you coming I thought you were dumb,' said Patrick shyly.

Flann laughed.

'That's a good trick. Let the other man talk. It never fails! I was ready to give him five gold pieces for you. Eat up! Another bowl if you wish. We must travel fast if we would reach Melcho's dun before the wolves begin to howl!'

Patrick was ready for a second bowl. He had never eaten such soup or bread. But he had never been so hungry before.

Flann stuck his thumbs in his belt and stretched his legs. He was ready to talk now.

'The gods alone know what Melcho will say, or shout, when he sees the long, lanky Roman I'm bringing him, instead of a short, sturdy Pict, or Briton. But I had to buy you! As I came through the market there was a whispering in my ear, "Buy the Roman with the one sandal! Buy the Roman with the one sandal!" Now what could that mean?'

Patrick pushed away his bowl.

'Set me free!' he pleaded. 'Give me a chance to escape. When I get back to my people my father will send you enough gold to buy two, or three slaves. Set me free!'

Flann shook his head.

'My poor lad, I dare not! Melcho would have my life! And who knows if your father still lives? By all accounts 'twas the fiercest raid known, and the raiders do not leave a job half done. Now cheer up. To be a slave is hard, but I have been to Rome and there I saw slaves fight with lions and tigers, and with one another in the arena to amuse Romans. We do not treat slaves that way in this country!'

Patrick scarcely listened to him.

'Let me go!' he urged. 'Even if my father is dead, which God forbid, there are other Romans who will reward you.'

Flann stared at him.

'Who is your God? You do not call on the gods I heard of in Rome.'

'I am a Christian!' Patrick told him. 'I worship the one true God!'

Flann stared at him with interest.

'I've met Christians before,' said Flann, leaning his elbows on the table. 'There were many in Rome. They did not worship Jupiter or Venus, or even Diana! And they never visited the arena. Sometimes, you know, they were persecuted themselves. I believe there are some in this country – in the south. One day, when we have more time, you shall tell me of your God. But now we must be moving.'

Patrick argued no more. He saw the raiders sitting in tents feasting and singing. Others were spending their money on jewelled rings and brooches, and one staggered by with an armful of silk robes.

'Hurry, Roman! Hurry!' commanded Flann.

Yet he stopped at a booth where bales of cloth were stacked on a wooden floor, carefully swept and polished.

The dealer came out, smiling and hoping he had a good customer.

He unrolled a length of bright red, woollen stuff which Patrick thought beautiful. Flann shook his head.

'Good thick cloth for winter gowns!' he snapped.

A narrow piece of green, loosely woven and with flecks of yellow, was then brought forward. Flann shook his head once more.

Soon billows of cloth, all colours and thicknesses, swirled up in front of the booth. Women, looking for winter garments, stood watching.

Others, carrying dripping baskets of fish, were toiling up from the river. A man, pushing a cart loaded with rough spearheads, paused beside Flann and stared down at a piece of smooth, crimson cloth.

'If I were a rich man I'd carry that home with me and we'd all go clad like nobles for a year or more,' he said enviously, then strode onward, grumbling at his poverty.

Patrick stepped back. A lane opened in the crowd and he could see the river straight ahead. He was a good runner, a fine swimmer. Once across, he would be safe.

He took one step away from the booth.

'Roman! Carry this bale!' called Flann without turning his head.

The boy hesitated. A horseman, horse and rider glittering with gold, rode by. Swaying from side to side came a painted chariot. Two sailors, dancing and laughing, knocked against him. Patrick could no longer see the river. He stepped forward.

'The purple cloth!' Flann pointed.

Patrick, with an effort, swung the bale to his shoulder.

'Never think to escape,' said Flann. 'There are wolves in the forest. You would be swallowed up in the bog unless you knew the paths. On the road you would be known for a runaway Roman slave. Come!'

He strode on. At the edge of the fairground a loaded cart, guarded by two small, dark men, stood waiting. The short, shaggy horse was munching a pile of cut grass. Obeying Flann's nod, Patrick placed the bale of cloth in the centre of the cart among bundles wrapped in coarse linen and wine jars fixed in nests of straw.

Flann sprang to the driver's seat and picked up the reins. He gave a sharp whistle. The horse shook its head, scattered the heap of grass and swung off.

Holding on at either side, the two small men managed to keep up. Patrick had learned to run against dogs and horses. He was refreshed now and, with his elbows close to his sides, his head flung back, he fell into a regular easy trot.

They went north from the river, away from the market where he had been sold. Sharp and quick on the road the horse's hooves rapped out at him, 'Roman slave! Roman slave! No escape! No escape!'


*Roman Slave*


Chariots and fine horsemen were on the road, carts like their own, and poor travellers on foot. As they drew north, duns hidden among trees, or rising above rocks, gathered in the other travellers, until they had the road to themselves.

They came to a river where rain had raised the level of the water so that the horse had to swim the ford. The two men and Patrick perched themselves on a plank sticking out at the back of the cart, their feet dangling. Patrick could see patches of corn and barley in clearings among the trees. He thought of the apple orchard and the great cider press at the back of his father's farm.

The road now crossed a bog, with narrow paths criss-crossing over it and pools covered with bright green weed. Low bushes, thick with purple berries, grew out from the heather, and bog cotton on thin, wiry stems fluttered in the wind.

A wide river had to be crossed on a huge raft, with room for carts and horses, which two men poled across. By listening carefully, Patrick was already learning a few words of the language these strangers spoke. He said them over and over again to himself.

'I'll need all the knowledge I can get if I am to escape,' he thought, for he was determined not to remain a slave.

Now the forest rose on each side. They left the high road and followed a narrow track which wound among rocks and so twisted that at times they seemed to be journeying south.

Patrick felt he could not run another step when Flann stopped the horse and jumped down from the cart.

The sun was still above the trees, and Flann had chosen a sloping bank where rocks poked up from the grass. He brought out a brown, flat loaf from under the seat and a jar of sweet yellow mead. He broke the loaf into four, and drinking from the jar, handed it to the older of the two men. Patrick drank last, but he did not mind that, nor the dregs. He was so thirsty he imagined the mead was finer than the best cider he had ever tasted. The bread was crisp and nutty, and when Flann sprang to his feet, the boy was so rested he was eager to hurry on.

Darkness came on the road while there was still faint light in the tree-tops. Flann shouted at the horse and cracked his whip so that the sturdy little animal galloped along the level road. Patrick began to drop behind, but he caught up again when the path climbed the slope of a mountain.

There was no thought of escape now in the young Roman's mind. He could hear a strange howling in the forest like a winter wind. He saw the frightened looks the small men cast at each side of the road.

'Hold fast to the cart!' ordered Flann. 'Do not lag behind!'

He spoke to Patrick. The others needed no telling.

Whichever way the boy looked there were mountain peaks rising into the air, chill and desolate. They went slowly now, up, up, towards the red glow of fires and the flickering light of torches. The barking of dogs came to them instead of the howling of wolves, and though it sounded fierce and threatening, Patrick heard it like a welcome.

'Home!' cried Flann. 'The dun of Melcho, Chief in Dalaradia,' he told Patrick.

Patrick, shivering in the cold wind which blew from the north, stared at the high, earthen wall rising before them. A wide, wooden door stood open and two men drove through a herd of cattle.

Patrick followed the cart beyond the wall, across a grassy space, through a gate in another wall into a great enclosure, crowded with buildings.

Flann stopped the horse at the entrance to a lofty hall with big doors. Patrick could see a raised platform at the far end, with a low, square table. Servants were arranging steaming dishes of meat, a cauldron of soup and wooden platters piled with round, flat cakes. He had never seen such a profusion of food in his more elegant Roman home. A long, narrow table of planks on trestles reached from the platform down the length of the hall, and fighting men were trooping in, leaning their spears and shields against the wall, to take their seats upon the wooden benches, opposite the women already seated there. A fire of trimmed logs blazed on an open hearth, and all along the walls flared lighted torches.

Patrick was hungry again, and the delightful smells of roast and boiled meat made him wonder how slaves were fed at Melcho's dun.

Through the doorway he could see into the huts and open sheds built against the earthen walls and larger houses ranged in half-circles.

The two small men began to unload the cart. They carried the jars of wine to the platform where a man in a green tunic and an embroidered cloak, thrown back from his shoulders, paced restlessly up and down. His thick, dark hair was bound with a circlet of gold, and the big brooch which fastened his cloak was purple with gems.

At a sign from Flann, Patrick lifted out the bale of cloth and carried it up to the platform.

'Unroll the bale!' ordered Flann. 'Let my Lord Melcho see the stuff, the thickest weave and the richest colour in the market.'

Patrick obeyed, draping the stuff over his arm as he had seen sellers of cloth do at his father's villa.

'This is the new slave, a Roman,' continued Flann. 'He is strong and young, and well taught.'

Melcho was sipping the wine. He did not look at the boy.

'So long as he guards my sheep and swine I care not

whether he be Pict or Roman,' he growled. 'The wine is good, Flann, but too sweet. The cloth is well woven, but my lady does not like dark colours. Were there no cloths with threads of gold or silver, or with strange patterns in bright threads?'

'The markets aren't what they used to be!' declared Flann. 'People want strength and thickness, not beauty. And when the snow falls and the river is frozen, there'll be great praise for Flann who brought such warm, comforting stuff into the dun.'

'You talk too much!' interrupted Melcho. 'And to think I hired you because you were nick-named the Silent One!'

Flann laughed, but became suddenly serious as a tall woman in a crimson gown, her long, fair hair falling over her shoulders and below her waist, pushed aside a heavy curtain and came into the hall. She wore a wide collar of beaten gold, so worked that it looked like lace, and thick gold bracelets on both arms. The warriors greeted her by standing up and beating on their shields with their spears.

She came over to where Patrick still held up the cloth and smiled at Flann.

'The stuff is both fine and warm!' she declared. 'You have done well, Flann.'

She looked down at Patrick.

'And this is the new slave?'

'A Roman, and only three pieces of gold!' boasted Flann. 'He would be wasted minding the sheep or swine. Yet I would trust him as I would myself.'

Melcho turned his back and sat down at the table.

'Let the slave start his work at dawn!' he ordered, speaking over his shoulder.

His wife sat down beside him.

'Do not be too hard on the boy, Melcho,' she said softly. 'He is young and has never known hardship.'

Flann motioned Patrick to return to the end of the hall. The boy went back to the door and stood there looking out.

The moon was rising, so bright he could see all over the enclosure. From the hut where the food was cooked a continuous stream of serving men and women came carrying fresh dishes and well-filled jugs. The huge wolfhounds wandered about or lay under the tables gnawing bones.

A woman put her hand on Patrick's shoulder and spoke to him. He did not understand. But she pressed him down to a low seat, gave him a plate piled with hot meat and put a wooden cup, filled with mead, on the floor beside him.

'I wish I could thank you,' he said, smiling up at her.

She smiled back, and Patrick was satisfied.

He had been so cold, hungry and tired, that to sit eating and drinking in that dark, warm corner was happiness. He could see and feel the leaping flames of the fire, see the bright light shining on the golden ornaments and rich clothes of Melcho and his wife. He stretched his legs and leaned against the wall.

At home he would have been with his father and mother, his young brother and his elder sister in a pillared hall, with thick rugs on a mosaic floor. There would be silver lamps on the table, and hot air in hidden pipes would keep them warm. Instead of the noise and confusion around him, slaves would move silently.

He closed his eyes and tried to shut out the strange voices.

A sudden silence roused him. The talkers had ceased as though stricken dumb. Not a dish rattled. Even in the cooking hut there was silence.

An old man at the high table pushed back his seat and taking a harp which leaned against the wall, swept his fingers over the strings.

The harper tossed back his long, white hair and sang. Though Patrick did not understand one word he felt excited and happy. Some of the men hammered the table with their fists. Others, seizing their spears, turned and beat on their bronze shields in time to the singing.

Melcho, red-faced and glaring, his blue eyes flashing, leaned sideways in the big chair with carved arms and a broad leather strap across its back.

'That must be a grand song!' said Patrick out loud.

Flann, leaning against the wall, heard him.

'That was a song of Finn Mac Cool. A great man, Finn! You never heard such music or singing in your land, Roman slave!'

Patrick was silent.

The harper played without singing – a sad little tune which made his listeners sigh and shake their heads. Patrick shared their sadness. He thought of his lost home and his lost freedom.

Again the old man sang, and now they were all laughing and singing with him. Melcho's children danced down the hall and back again. They looked gay and friendly, and Patrick longed to know them.

Suddenly Melcho stood up. He pulled the circlet of gold from his head and placed it on the old harper's white hair. All the fighting men, the women, the slaves, shouted in delight, and Patrick shouted with them.

That night Patrick slept with other boys on the floor of the hall. There were rushes on the ground and the fire kept them warm, but the young Roman had been used to a raised bed with linen sheets and a pillow for his head.

He woke before dawn to hear the distant howling of wolves and the answering cries of hounds which kept guard between the two walls.

A great cauldron of hot soup thickened with barley was carried in by two men. The boys had wooden bowls and served themselves again and again until the big black pot was empty.

Flann came in with a young hound on a leash. He beckoned Patrick.

'Here is your comrade,' he said. 'Melcho's lady gives him to you. 'Tis she has the kind heart!'

Patrick laid his hand fearlessly on the big, rough head. The hound sniffed at him and moved closer.

'A good beginning!' declared Flann. 'Come! Your work lies yonder. Aedh, the herd, is a coward. He has lost many sheep and swine to the wolves, even a precious hound, for he cannot manage animals. Tomorrow he goes back to his old task of carrying water. Today he will teach you.'

The sun was rising over the mountains, but along the valley a thick mist hid the river, though Patrick could hear it dashing against rocks and falling into pools. As they came to a bare hillside where sheep were feeding on the short, sweet grass, a boy of Patrick's age rushed down to meet them. His hair was matted, his arms and legs caked with mud, and he looked at Patrick without friendliness.

Flann led the way to a small hut built in the shelter of rocks. The back was solid rock, the side stones piled on one another, and the roof a single slab. Before the opening a fire smouldered. Inside, a heap of dry leaves served for a bed. A pot which could be placed on the fire and a jar of water stood in one corner, a spear in the other.

'You will live here,' said Flann.

He saw Patrick's look of dismay and gave the lad a slap on the shoulder.

'A slave's life is hard, surely. But Melcho is proud of his swine and prouder still of his flocks. Guard them well and, who can tell, you may end up as a fighting man, or servant to a Druid. I have known many a slave win freedom that way!'

'I could not be servant to a Druid. I am Christian!' declared Patrick.

Flann shook his head.

'The Druids are powerful. And who could wish a grander god than the sun!'

'The sun is grand and wonderful,' agreed Patrick. 'So is the moon, and the earth itself, but God made them all!'

Flann looked at him kindly.

'I think well of you, lad, for standing by your own god. Yet keep a still tongue. Learn by me that there's a time to be silent and a time to talk. Melcho has no liking for those who disagree with him, and he is a great believer in the Druids. Listen to me now. There are 500 sheep, 100 swine. They were counted the last day of the big moon. You must follow their tracks and keep the sheep this side of the mountain, the swine this end of the forest. Never must they be found in the corn or barley fields. And never let your fire go out. Build it up each night with these sods of the bog earth. That is your great safeguard against the wolves. Remember – each big moon your herd and flocks are counted. If there is one missing, if there are not the usual number of lambs and young swine – you will be beaten and set to cleaning, or carrying water like Aedh here.'

Aedh crouched beside the fire. Patrick shivered, for his tunic was thin, and the morning air damp and cold.

'Aedh will show you the ways through the forest, and how to cut and dry the burning earth,' said Flann. 'But tomorrow you will be alone with the young hound. When you need food come to the dun. But do not come too often. Melcho likes his slaves to be at their posts.'

He strode away. Patrick ran after him.

'I will see you again?' he asked anxiously.

Flann sighed.

'I do not stay at the dun. I am always on the road, buying and selling for Melcho. But I always return. So we shall meet again. And I shall always be your friend, young Roman!'

Patrick stared after Flann until his short, broad figure vanished through the entrance to the dun. Then he turned back to the sulky lad who sat watching him.

Aedh stood up. The sooner he showed this stranger the work to be done, the sooner he could go to the warmth and safety of the walled fort.

He led the way into the forest.

The young Roman was glad of the hound, which kept step with him as they went into the shade of the trees. Aedh showed the oaks where the swine gathered, feeding on the ripe acorns as they dropped to the grass, and the giant beeches with the thick carpet of beech mast among the roots. The boars were fierce and distrustful, and the hound was ready to spring at them. Aedh drove the savage creatures with a switch and, to Patrick's surprise, they trotted off, grunting.

'How in the wide world can I count them?' he thought.

They came out from the forest and followed the sheep tracks. Patrick soon learned that, though the hound was supposed to hunt wolves, it knew more of the ways of sheep than he did. Still, he held on to the leash.

'When we know one another better, you shall go as free as I,' he said.

He couldn't talk to Aedh. Yet by the time they returned to the hut there was friendship between them.

Aedh took out a sharp knife hidden under a piece of rope, and with Patrick and the hound following him, climbed down to a patch of bog. He led the way to a strip where the rough grass and heather had been burned away, and began to cut blocks from the soft brown earth. He spread these out where they would be dried by wind and sun, and showed a pile of dry sods he had already built up.

He tied about a dozen sods together with the rope and, giving the load to Patrick to carry, went back to the hut.

Aedh brought out the pot, which was filled with soup, and placed it on the hot ashes. Flann had left them a cake of bread and, when the soup was ready, he broke this into it. Seated side by side the boys spooned out the food and Patrick put a share of his on the earth for the hound.

By this time Aedh was wishing he could stay. With Patrick for his companion the wolves would not be so terrifying.

Aedh left before dark. Now Patrick had only the hound and the fire to keep him from loneliness. In the distance was the lighted dun and overhead the stars.

At night the hound slept with Patrick, keeping him warm, and by day they worked together. The swine and the sheep had never been so guarded before, yet Melcho had no word of praise for the Roman slave.

Melcho was a fierce, angry man, always at war with other chiefs, and he hated the tall, serious boy who walked into the dun as though he were a king's son. The tyrant resented the influence Patrick had over the other slaves and over his own children. The hounds followed meekly as he passed through the gate, and the children rushed to meet him.

The two little girls and the boy went to his hut among the rocks and, sitting at his turf fire, coaxed him to tell where he had lived before and how he had become a slave.

Patrick told them his story. He told them that he was a Christian, and when they asked him what that meant he tried to explain, but he couldn't answer half their questions.

'If only I knew more!' he cried. 'The years I wasted! But – one day I shall be free and then I'll learn everything!'

He was no longer lonely. He was ragged, for Melcho grudged him a tunic, and often hungry, for he forgot food. But the children and the faithful hound were his friends. Even the blackbirds, nesting in the thicket on the lower bank of the river, knew him. In those silent nights on Slemish Patrick learned to pray. Sometimes a great happiness came to him. Yet still he longed for freedom.

Once, before dawn, when a blackbird was singing to itself, he heard a voice calling and started up.

'Who calls Patrick?' he cried.

'Soon you will return to your own country!' was the answer.

Patrick stared about him. He was alone. The dun was in darkness and in silence except for one hound, which

73

barked at long intervals. He could hear the stream, swollen with rain, pouring over rocks, down to the Lagan. Patrick wondered if he had been dreaming, but he had not been asleep.

Another night he sat by his fire, thinking of the voice which had spoken to him. A mist, so thick he could see nothing outside the light of the fire, shut him in. Suddenly he heard the voice again – 'Patrick! Your ship is ready!'

He did not hesitate one moment. Fastening the thongs of his rough sandals securely, he raced down the path. Even in the mist he could not take a false step. He knew that path too well. After him came the hound.

'Go back, faithful friend!' said Patrick. 'This is your home, guard the sheep until Melcho sends another herd.'

Whimpering and sorrowful, the hound returned, while the Roman slave set out on his journey to the coast.

He was very unlike the boy who had passed along these roads from the slave market with Flann. He was six years older – tall, thin, tanned with wind and sun. He could speak Gaelic now and had almost forgotten his Latin. He had grown used to being a slave, but now he understood the value of freedom.

### Escape

All through the night Patrick kept to the road. He heard the howling of wolves and the crashing of wild boars among the trees, but he dared not stop. If he were not out of Melcho's territory by morning he might be overtaken and brought back.

When morning came he had reached the ferry. He had

no money, but there was such a crowd waiting for the big raft that he squeezed on board unnoticed.

As they crossed, the other passengers stared at him. His rags were those of a slave, but his dignity and silence made them wonder.

'I must be careful!' he thought. 'But Melcho will not dream I am gone for hours, even for a whole day!'

He was now on the great road to Tara. When horsemen or chariots came along he hid in the woods, but at noon he stopped where a tree had been cut down. In a clearing just beyond he could see a hut made of branches thrust in the ground, fastened at the top and plastered with mud.

A woodman was roasting a salmon on a fire outside the hut and as Patrick came slowly from the road, through the trees, the man watched him.

When the runaway came nearer and the woodman could see his face, he nodded with satisfaction.

'You're in time!' he called. 'The salmon is just browned!'

He broke it in two and placed half on a flat piece of wood.

'Eat up, stranger. You're very welcome!'

'God reward you!' said Patrick, eating the salmon.

He fell asleep while the woodman was gathering chips to build up the fire and woke to find that rain was falling, but he was sheltered by an arched branch, which had been placed over him.

'I must be on my way!' he declared, jumping up so that he sent the branch flying.

The woodman was as sorry to see him go as if they had been friends for years, and he remained staring after Patrick when he was far down the road.

Now he crossed a bog and the wind from the mountains

beat in his face. He came to another river. He could not see a ferry. There were no fishermen's boats. He stood on the bank, the cold rain streaming over him, and waited.

From out a clump of reeds came a queer, round boat made of willow twigs twisted in and out, and covered with hide. A lad worked the boat with one paddle, and he brought it in to where the runaway slave stood ankle deep in mud.

'I cannot pay you,' said Patrick. 'I am a runaway slave!'

'Two can cross as easy as one,' the lad told him. 'And 'tis a lonesome day. You're the first since dawn!'

When they reached the opposite bank he pushed the coracle under an overhanging tree and the paddle under his arm.

'There's a pot of stew,' he said, sniffing, 'and only me mother and meself to eat it. Come along, friend!'

The boy and his mother lived in a hut of sods thatched with rushes. It was snug and neat. A wide bed of beech boughs spread with a soft hide made a comfortable seat, and the stew was savoury. The three of them sat side by side eating from the one pot.

He told them of his early life and his slavery.

'You look good!' said the woman. 'And you must be loved by the gods.'

'There is only one God!' said Patrick. 'I am a Christian. And I'd want you to be Christians too, if only I knew more!'

They asked him questions until he fell asleep. When he set off again the mother went with him to the next river and showed him a ford with stepping stones used by very few so that he would not be seen. She gave him a cake made of ground hazel nuts and made him promise to come back one day.

He was growing tired when he saw a party of men armed with battleaxes running along the road. He climbed into a tree and watched them as he wondered were they bound for Melcho's dun. Propped against the trunk he fell asleep, and when he woke the road was once more deserted.

Patrick passed a dun so hidden by high rocks that only the hounds on guard showed him where it lay. They came leaping along the craggy path threatening to drag him down. But the first to reach him crouched at his feet, and, as they came up, the others stood round, friendly and welcoming.

A slave followed them, a slave who herded swine in the forest, and he took Patrick to his hut.

'You're a friend to hounds, that's easy seen!' declared the man. 'They're the fiercest between here and Tara!'

He had no fire, but he gave Patrick cold meat and beer made from wild herbs. He had no interest in anything but swine and hounds, and never troubled to go as far as the road.

The road crossed a plain, yet still Patrick could find shelter in the woods. Now he saw a dim chain of mountains rising beyond the misty fields.

He knew one more river barred his way. He followed a man driving a cart loaded with wooden dishes and platters. The man leaned down and looked at Patrick. He liked the runaway's clear eyes and had pity for his thin body and poor rags.

'Climb up: ye're footsore!' said the driver. 'There's room here beside me. 'Tis a quiet road and a bit of sensible talk never did a man harm.'

Patrick could sing a song or tell a story, and he longed to ask where he would find a ship. But he remembered Flann's silence. If he asked questions he might be suspected. And this friendly man would perhaps tell him all he wanted to know without being asked.

'I've a grand load here!' declared the driver. 'Did ye ever see better carving or painting? The carved ones are the best, though that's good paint, the best of paint. 'Tis me daughter's work. She won a bag of gold for it at the Tara Feis last year. I shaped the wood for her. I'm making for a ship that should be coming up from the Inland Sea with wine and silks. There's a ford here. Hold tight now! And don't lie back on me dishes!'

The horse went slowly down the bank and plunged into the dark water which only half covered the wheels, for they were near the sea and the tide was out.

'Were ye ever this way before?' asked the driver. 'They call it the dark pool.' (Now it is Dublin on the Liffey.)

Patrick shook his head. He had never been so far south.

On the banks the hawthorn bushes were bright with berries and a flock of birds rose from them as the horse plunged up from the water and climbed the bank.

'Ye should be here when the bushes are in flower,' said the driver. 'Their full, sweet smell will travel a mile or more.'

The horse splashed across a path of flat stones laid on the marshy soil.

'Why don't ye come with me as far as the ship?' asked Patrick's companion. 'I like a pleasant talker. There's times when I don't hear a bit of news for a week. My workshop is away from the road and no travellers pass by. I can see ye like birds though I prefer horses, and ye've a look about ye of a man that likes dogs and children. Ah, there's nothing like a bit of good chat. No doubt about it, ye're a good talker!'

Patrick smiled, for he had been making a great effort to

keep silent and not ask questions. They followed the coast now, and when Patrick saw the waves blue in the sunshine and their white-crested tips he wondered would he hear again the voice which had sent him on his journey or should he ask for help from this friendly, talkative stranger.

They rested on the bank of a narrow river where two men were mending a boat. The maker of wooden vessels had brought his tools with him and Patrick was strong, so they were of great help and the boat was soon finished. Then they shared a pot of fish boiled with herbs and the half of a jar of wine.

On they went, taking to the sandy shore where shells crushed under the wheels and long-legged crabs scuttled into pools or hid behind rocks.

'If I were a good-looking, well-spoken young fella like ye,' said the driver, 'I'd go on a ship and see the world. Look! There's the harbour, and Mananan be praised, me vessel is in! If ye're looking for a ship ye'll find shelter in yonder hut until ye're served. Tell them ye're a friend of mine. They'll not drive ye away! May ye have good fortune!'

To Patrick's surprise the driver seemed now in a hurry to be rid of him, so he slipped to the ground.

'Listen!' said the man suddenly, leaning down and speaking in a whisper. 'I can tell ye're a runaway slave and ye might meet those who aren't as easy-going as I am. Wait until night before ye look for a ship, if that's yer wish. Until then ye'll be safe yonder.'

'God reward you for your kindness!' said Patrick.

There were three ships in the harbour. One was unloading jars of wine, and soon it would be taking on the wooden bowls as well as the ingots of gold and bars of copper ranged on the quayside and guarded by watchful men armed with long swords. Farther on he saw baskets of coloured beads and pieces of smoked meat wrapped in grass, but the third ship seemed deserted.

'That is the ship I must journey in,' thought Patrick, as sure as if he had been told.

Other ships were sailing into the harbour, and boats rowed by two or three banks of oarsmen. Carts piled high with sacks of grain, jars of mead and bundles wrapped in cloth, came up from the three roads which led to the harbour. In spite of the haste and confusion, curious eyes grew suspicious as Patrick walked up from the strand, and he knew that his friend had been wise in telling him to keep out of sight.

Night was coming on but there was still light enough for the work of loading and unloading, and for strangers to be noticed. Patrick walked past a line of huts beyond the storing sheds. Outside the last of them, the one which the driver had shown him, an old man and an old woman were mending a net. A little boy sat near them trying to build a house with pebbles. His hands were unsteady and no sooner had he three layers on one another than down they fell.

Patrick knelt beside the child and showed him how to build a wall. The old people sat watching. Soon there were four walls, with a gap for the door. Then Patrick laid a flat stone on top and the house was complete.

'I lived in one like that, only bigger, for six years,' he said.

The little boy looked at him with wonder.

'Where are you from, young stranger?' asked the old man. 'And where are you going?'

'I come from the north in search of a ship,' Patrick told him.

The old man looked at the young man's lean, brown

body, his ragged tunic and the sandals which were worn to strips. He whispered to his wife.

'If you are travelling,' she said, 'you need shoes to keep your feet from the hard road and a garment to save you from being shrivelled by the sea winds. Come with me!'

Patrick followed her into the hut. From a big, wooden chest she brought out a pair of stout sandals, a tunic of green wool and a thick cloak.

'I am a runaway slave,' said Patrick, 'and I am a Christian.'

The old woman still held out the clothes towards him.

'You are not the first runaway slave we have helped,' she told him. 'It is a cruel, wicked thing to own slaves. Take the clothes! They belonged to the father of the child you were playing with. The sea took him from his boat in the last storm. He would give them to you gladly, for he was a Christian too!'

Patrick took the clothes. He had not been so well dressed since he became a slave.

'There's a deal of kindness in the world!' he declared.

'There's a deal of kindness in yourself, young man, I'm thinking!' returned the old woman. 'Now we'll be sharing a pot of broth and a piece of cheese. Then we'll talk over what you should do.'

It was dark before they finished eating. Patrick told them all about himself, and there wasn't a word from them until he said he must go on that ship which was lying silent and deserted while the shouting of sailors, singing, and the thudding of dancing feet came from all along the quays.

'That's the ship that takes the big wolfhounds,' said the old man. 'They're a wild, rough lot, neither Christian nor

pagan, but just heathen. They bring the hounds themselves, sail the ship and have no friends here or anywhere
else.'

'That is the ship I must go by!' said Patrick.

'But you'll come back?' asked the old woman.

'I'll come back!' promised Patrick.

'We aren't Christians, but my son was and so will the
child be if he has the chance,' said the old man. 'We have
no teaching. The Christians are scattered and the Druids
have all the power and learning in the country. We need
teachers, we need learning. If we had them, we would be
Christians too.'

'I will come back,' said Patrick. 'But not until I have
learnt all I can.'

They were still talking when, looking out, Patrick saw
that there were men on board the deserted ship, tieing
the great leather sail to the mast and putting out the
oars.

From the central road came the whining and scuffling
of hounds, shouts and confused orders.

The three of them rushed out and saw a crowd of men
and boys urging a long string of the big wolfhounds down
to the harbour.

The animals were savage, for the men were beating
them unmercifully, and Patrick felt he must interfere.

He hurried towards them, then turned back.

'I go with the hounds,' he told the old man and
woman.

Then off he went, while they shouted farewell and
Godspeed.

By this time the hounds could see the water. They
strained and reared against the cords which fastened
them, and snapped at the men, who were too alarmed to
do anything but use their sticks.

'We'll never get these beasts on board!' cried one man.

'I'll manage them!' said Patrick, and, pushing the leader on one side, he caught the collar of the largest hound.

At once it ceased snarling, and when Patrick stepped to the plank which led from the quayside to the deck of the ship, it went with him meekly, the others following as gently as sheep.

Patrick saw now that the hold was filled with iron cages, ready for the hounds. Obeying him they went in one after the other until all the hounds were on board and the cages filled.

The captain watched in amazement, but he was a mean, surly man.

'What are you wanting?' he growled. 'Remember I did not ask you to do this.'

'Let me on your ship,' replied Patrick. 'I can row. I am good with animals. I need little food and I can speak Latin.'

The captain glared.

'I want no runaway slaves on my ship!' he shouted. 'You offer too much for too little. I know these cheap shipmen. You and your Latin! For all I know you may be a Christian too! Off with you!'

'I am a Christian!' declared Patrick, and he stepped off the ship.

As he walked away he was dismayed. He had been so sure this was the ship that would carry him to freedom. He had been wrong. If wrong in this, might he not have been wrong before? Had he really heard that voice upon Mount Slemish? He had come all this way. He had left behind the only place he knew.

'And all this time I've been coming to believe I was the

one to bring Christianity to this land! I've been foolish. What can I do?'

He was half-way to the hut when a terrible clamour arose on the ship he had left.

'Are they beating those hounds again?' he thought indignantly.

'Hi! Hi! Come back!'

A boy was running after him, shouting as he came.

Patrick turned.

'Captain says you're to come!' panted the boy. 'Hurry! They're casting off! Tide's on the turn!'

Patrick raced back to the harbour. Already the oars were splashing in the water and there was a widening strip between the ship and the quay. He gave a leap that sent him flying through the air but he landed on the deck and kept his feet.

'Take an oar, Christian runaway!' ordered the captain. 'I'll see you earn your passage!'

### Days of Wandering

Guided by the stars, the ship of dogs crossed the sea. On calm days Patrick toiled at the oars, fed the dogs and made friends with the sailors. They told him this was the best voyage they had ever made.

'We always carry the great wolfhounds,' the steersman told him, 'and they howl and snarl from one shore to t'other! This time a man would think we brought a cargo of lambs.'

'Where will they be sold?'

'The hounds are for Rome to fight wolves in the arena,' the man told him. 'They're a cruel lot, those Romans!'

'Yet isn't Rome the most wonderful city in the world?' asked Patrick.

As the hills of Erin grew dim in the distance Patrick leaned over the stern of the ship and watched until he could see only waves and never a sight of land. He no longer thought of Rome. He had been a slave. Often he had been half-starved. Now he had won his freedom and the world lay before him. Yet already he was planning to return.

'I will come back!' he cried.

'All exiles say that,' the steersman told him with a grin.

'I have something to come back for!' said the escaped slave.

He no longer dreamed of boasting that he was a Roman. Ireland had become his country.

The voyage was so easy that even the sullen captain was satisfied. After the third day the oars were shipped and in the shadow of the swelling sail, the men lay singing or telling stories. Patrick listened until his turn came. He told them how he had been a child in Roman Britain, of the raid which had swept him into slavery and of the voice which had led him to freedom.

'But you're going back, back to the land of your slavery!' said the steersman.

'I am going back,' agreed Patrick. 'I am going to take Christianity into every dun in Erin!'

Now the rocky coast of Gaul came into view. The sail was taken down and the men put out the oars. The captain stood by the mast watching anxiously. He could see the harbour, but it was empty. None of the boats which usually crowded it were there. Beyond the rocks which marked the entrance and hanging low over the water, was a pall of smoke. As they drew nearer they could see smouldering ruins where once had been the buildings of a great port. But the port was gone.

A single boat put out to meet them. The Vandals had sacked the town and the traders, who would have bought the hounds, had fled.

'Then I'll follow them!' cried the captain. 'Am I to have all my labour for nothing? Where have they gone?'

No one could tell him that.

'Wolfhounds are wanted everywhere!' declared the captain. 'I'll take them to the next town. If necessary I'll take them to Rome itself!'

The ship entered the harbour. Leaving the steersman and half the sailors on board to wait his return, the captain, with the six remaining sailors and the hounds, commenced their march along the inland road.

'How about you, Christian slave?' asked the captain.

'I'm with you,' replied Patrick, 'even to Rome!'

The captain was thankful to have him, for he secretly dreaded that journey with the valuable but savage animals.

The road was empty. They came to a village; the houses were untouched, but not one human being remained to welcome them or even to run from the little company in terror. Day after day they went through a plundered countryside, where cornfields were trampled down, wells destroyed. On the horizon they saw the smoke of burning towns and forts. They camped among ruins and began to wonder if all the people were taken prisoner or were hiding in the mountains.

They had brought provisions with them from the ship, but at last these were all eaten and the wine jars were empty. There was no food for the hounds and they whined miserably as they followed Patrick.

'Now, Christian,' jeered the captain, 'you think your God powerful. Why not pray to him for food? If he cannot help us we shall perish in this desert.'

The sailors were lying by the side of the road, too weak to march any further. Only the captain stood erect, and he was stronger than most men.

'God is very merciful!' said Patrick.

He knelt at the side of the road and prayed. The hounds lay all round him. The sailors watched anxiously.

As he stood up, a herd of swine crossed the road.

'After them!' cried the captain.

Off went the hounds and the men, and that night they made a fire in a ruined house and ate roasted meat.

The next morning one of the sailors found a hollow tree filled with wild honey, such a store of it that they were able to load all their wine jars.

They were in sight of the town where the captain hoped he would sell the hounds, when down the road came marching a company of Vandals. They were so wild and savage that even the captain was terrified. There was no chance of escape. Once again Patrick was a captive. With the captain and the sailors he carried great loads of booty, fixed tents, built fires and burnished weapons. But, during a fight in the mountains, Patrick escaped, determined never to be recaptured.

Now he wandered through Gaul and came to Italy. He worked and told stories for his living. He longed to return home though he feared he would be forgotten. He wondered if he would again see that strange land where he had been a slave. Wherever he went there was fighting and desolation, but he met with more and more Christians, and while he wandered, he learned all he could.

At last he came to the island of Lerins, where all the people were Christians and a great monastery had been built. Here he became a monk and, as he paced the strand, praying and dreaming, he began to understand what he must do to carry out his mission.

He knew he must bring Christianity not to a few who knew and believed in him but to the whole nation – to the High King at Tara, the chiefs in their duns, peasants in their huts and the slaves who were bought and sold as he had been.

It was a long time before he had a chance to return to his own people. He was given a great welcome, though his father and mother were dead and many had forgotten him. The villas had been rebuilt. There were trading ships in the harbour, and a new church of stone had arisen close by the rock where Patrick had first seen the Irish raiders.

After all his wanderings among strangers Patrick found it pleasant to be home in peace and quiet.

One night he had a strange dream.

He saw a man who came from Ireland with many letters in his hand. He gave one of them to Patrick, who began to read it. At the top was written, *The Voice of the Irish*. As he read he could hear voices crying out to him, 'We entreat thee, holy youth, to come and walk once more among us!'

When Patrick awoke his mind was made up – he would delay no longer. First he must be prepared. He left home, this time willingly, though his people grieved to lose him. He went to Auxerre, a city of Gaul, which was the greatest centre of learning and piety in the West at that time. There he was ordained a deacon and there he had ten years of religious life, study and training. At one time Patrick reached Tours, where his uncle, Saint Martin, was bishop. The Bishop had a wattled cell, while the monks lived in holes in the cliff face above the valley. The cells were airy and dry, though little light entered. Outside was a level platform of rock, not more than ten feet wide and forty feet up from the road. Patrick studied here and was happier than he had been for years.

He heard that Palladius had been chosen to go to Ireland, but he was not discouraged. Palladius went to Ireland, but his mission was not successful and he returned. Patrick was made a bishop so that he could go with authority as the first Bishop of Ireland.

## The Return

When Patrick came back to Ireland he was no longer young, but the finest part of his life was before him. On the journey he talked to his companions of Melcho's dun with the mountains and the forest, the little patches of corn or barley, brown bogs with snow-white bog cotton and the strange mists. They were all as excited as Patrick himself when their ship came in sight of the Irish coast and the hills rose up over the sea. But when they tried to land, a hostile crowd drove them away.

Patrick had waited too long to be easily discouraged. He sailed farther north and made another landing to take fresh water on board. They made a camp, and while Patrick slept a young boy named Benen came up, curious to see the strangers. He had been picking flowers and he laid them beside the sleeping bishop.

'You must not do that!' exclaimed one of the Christians indignantly.

At the sound of his voice Patrick woke and saw the friendly boy.

'Do not be angry with him,' he said. 'One day this lad will be my heir!'

When they went back to their ship Benen's father allowed the boy to go too as Patrick's attendant, and, years after, he became Saint Benignus.

They passed by Connaile where Cuchulain had fought and hunted, by Cooley, the land of the Brown Bull. When they came to Strangford Lough, Patrick knew his voyage was ended. They landed and followed a path which led inland beside the Slaney. They were too tired to go farther when they reached a barn and took shelter.

The swineherd of Dichu, lord of the place, saw the strangers and rushed to give warning to his master that pirates had come ashore.

Dichu, a brave, impulsive man, came with his dog to resist the intruders. The huge creature leapt towards Patrick, but instead of harming him, stood up with its great paws on the bishop's shoulders and made friends with him.

So did his master, for, looking at Patrick, he knew that here was no robber, but a very noble man.

'You're not a pirate!' cried Dichu. 'What brings you here?'

'I am a Christian and I have come to bring Ireland the true faith,' replied Patrick. 'They have made me a bishop and my name is Patrick.'

'Come with me!' said Dichu. 'I have heard of Christians and nothing but good. You shall make a Christian of me. My dun is yours and here you shall build your first church.'

So Patrick built his first church at Saul, and Dichu's dun became known as the Dun of Patrick, or, as we now call it – Downpatrick.

'Now I will go to my old master,' said Patrick. 'He will

have forgotten me, for I have been away long years, but the children will remember me, so will Flann and Aedh.'

As they came in sight of Melcho's dun, Patrick felt as if he had been away only a day. But the hound who had been his comrade was dead, and the children he had played with were grown now like himself. Yet they remembered. Flann, too, who was old and liked best to sit by the fire telling stories of the young Roman without fear, came to welcome him.

Patrick had been a slave when they had last seen him. Now he came in the robes of a bishop. He had a powerful chieftain for friend, and the news of his coming had spread all over Ireland.

In all those years Melcho had cherished his hatred of Patrick. Now that he saw him free and independent he hated him more than ever. The proud chieftain would not listen to Patrick. He would not even see him, but shut himself up in his dun, though his wife, his children, Flann and his best warriors were among the first to be baptized Christians by Patrick.

## The Fire of Slane

'If you would make Ireland Christian you must go to Tara,' Dichu told Patrick. 'Only the High King can give you leave to preach the faith all through the country.'

'Then I will go to Tara!' said Patrick.

With eight of his party as well as young Benen, Patrick set sail up the River Boyne until they came to the hill of Slane. They climbed the hill and here, on Holy Saturday, Patrick pitched his tent.

'We shall celebrate Easter on Slane,' he said.

As darkness came on, Patrick struck a flint and lit the Paschal fire in honour of Easter. The tiny light shone through the darkness of the countryside until it was seen at Tara.

Below stretched the fertile plains of Meath, and far off rose the Mountains of Mourne.

The High King Laoghaire was at Tara with his Druids. They were keeping the pagan high festival of Rach, the god of fire, and walking in darkness. The law was that every light, every fire in the country must be put out until the fire was relit in the royal palace.

Suddenly Laoghaire saw a slender golden column of flame rising from the hill of Slane, over ten miles away.

'Who dares light a fire before me?' cried the King angrily.

'Unless yonder fire be put out this night,' declared the Chief Druid, 'he who lit it will reign over the whole of Ireland!'

'Then I will go to Slane and put it out!' exclaimed King Laoghaire.

With the Queen, his Druids, his horsemen and three times nine chariots, the King set out from Tara. First they rode circlewise to the left against the course of the sun. They had no light, not even from the stars, only the white road glimmering before them.

From beside his fire on the hill of Slane, Patrick heard the thunder of hoofs and a grinding of wheels upon the road.

'Hear the horsemen!' whispered Benen, who was trembling with excitement.

'Heap up the fire!' ordered Patrick.

Though still no light shone on Tara, from every valley and mountainside people watching saw the blaze on Slane.

The Druids advised the King to halt a mile from Slane so that the power of the fire could not harm him. A messenger was sent to Patrick bidding him come to Laoghaire.

As Patrick came down from the hill and walked slowly along the road King Laoghaire cried out – 'Seize that man!'

A great tumult arose in the darkness, a wind that flung over the chariots, while the horses dashed off, dragging them to destruction. The King's men, thinking they were attacked, fought with one another. Only three were left with Patrick – the King, Queen Angas and the Chief Druid.

Laoghaire was the son of Niall of the Nine Hostages, whose raid had changed Patrick's whole life. Niall had been a man of war, but Laoghaire loved peace. He was wise and generous, and, as he talked to Patrick at the foot of Slane, he knew that this daring stranger would bring no harm to Ireland. The Queen, too, was friendly.

But the Chief Druid realized that here was a power that would overthrow his, and he determined on Patrick's destruction.

Laoghaire made his decision.

'Tomorrow you shall come to Tara and we will hear you with all our Court!'

He wheeled his horses round and back to Tara went the royal chariot.

'Tomorrow,' said Patrick to his followers, 'we will take the Cross to Tara of the Kings!'

They were awake before dawn and the Bishop celebrated Mass in a little hut. Down through the mist they went to the River Boyne and crossed over in a coracle of wood and hide, which a fisherman had brought for them.

Patrick knew there was danger for, if he succeeded, the rule of the Druids was broken.

His companions were afraid, but they trusted him and to give them courage, he began to chant a hymn of protection –

'Christ with me, Christ before me;
Christ be after me, Christ within me;
Christ beneath me, Christ above me;
Christ at my right hand, Christ at my left;
Christ in the fort, Christ in the chariot-seat;
Christ in the ship;
Christ in the heart of every man who thinks of me;
Christ in the heart of every man who speaks of me;
Christ in every eye that sees me;
Christ in every ear that hears me.

I bind unto myself today
The virtues of the starlit heaven,
The glorious sun's life-giving ray,
The whiteness of the moon at even,
The flashing of the lightning free,
The whirling wind's tempestuous shocks,
The stable earth, the deep salt sea
Around the old eternal rocks.
I bind unto myself today
The power of God to hold and lead,
His eye to watch, His might to slay,
His ear to hearken to my need.

The wisdom of my God to teach,
His hand to guide, His shield to ward;
The word of God to give me speech,
His heavenly host to be my guard.'

They needed protection, for a body of armed men lay hidden at the cross-roads ready to attack them. From a distance the waiting men heard a strange cry, but instead of a Roman in white and purple robes, with his attendants, they saw a herd of deer gallop by and the strange chanting went with them. To this day that hymn is known as *The Deer's Cry* or *Saint Patrick's Breastplate*.

Now Patrick saw the roofs of Tara rising before him. Inside that vast enclosure were many duns. The finest house of all was a sunny building with a balcony – the grianan – which was reserved for women and girls. Near by was the dun built by Niall for his princely hostages.

Crowds had gathered along the road and they were massed outside the great banqueting hall. Inside, with the King and Queen, were the nobles, the Druids, the bards and harpers. Even before his coming some were friendly to Patrick and the new faith. The Chief Druid had ordered that no welcome or honour of any kind should be given Patrick, even though he came by the King's invitation. But as Patrick reached the door the chief poet, Erc, stood up and saluted the stranger. Fiace, his nephew, a poet too, also stood in Patrick's honour.

Guards were at the doors, and past them walked Patrick carrying the Cross as other Romans had carried the eagles of Rome.

He went straight up to the King.

'I have come, O King!'

'You are welcome!' replied Laoghaire.

The Chief Druid challenged Patrick to show his power.

'First, I will make a spell!' said the Druid.

Though the day was warm and sunny, snow began to fall. Patrick and his companions, King Laoghaire, Queen Angas, the nobles, pagans and Christians, free people and slaves, watched while the walls of the dun, the roofs of the halls, the bogs and woods beyond, were covered with a thick, white blanket of snow. Slowly the distant mountains were blotted out. The people began to shiver and complain. The nobles wrapped their cloaks about them. The slaves piled logs upon the fires, and still the snow fell.

'That is wonderful, but a foolish deed!' said Patrick. 'You have shown your power. Now take the snow away!'

'Till tomorrow the snow must remain!' declared the Druid.

'While the people freeze!' protested Queen Angas indignantly.

'You are potent for evil, not for good!' Patrick told the Druid.

He made the sign of the Cross. The snow ceased falling, the sun shone out and once more the brown of the bog, the blue of the distant mountains, could be seen, and the people cheered.

'The Roman is indeed a great man!' they told one another.

Though the day was still early the Druids brought a heavy darkness on the land. Patrick dispersed it. Every spell they wrought he defeated until he became angry and cried out that he had not come to measure one magic against another but to preach the Gospel and tell the people of Christ. Picking a shamrock, he held it up so that he might explain the Trinity. The Druids had to stay and listen, and some became Christians.

Queen Angas, too, became a Christian. But though Laoghaire believed Patrick was right, he remained a pagan.

'I will live as my father Niall of the Nine Hostages lived!' he declared. 'When I die I will be buried standing, my weapons in my hand, my face to the foe!'

Yet he willingly gave Patrick permission to go through

Ireland preaching and building churches. We can follow the saint's wanderings all over the country, north and south, east and west. Where he went he made friends as in the days when Flann and the children of Melcho loved him.

Keelta, one of the old Fenians, who had, it is said, lived on from the time of Finn Mac Cool, became his friend. With his help Patrick had the Brehon Laws rewritten, and Keelta told him the ancient stories of pagan times. The saint had these written down by his scribes, for he would not have anything fine or beautiful forgotten – this Roman who was the first bishop and the greatest saint of Ireland.

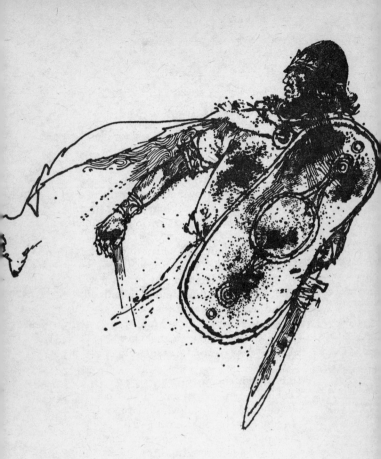

# 3

## ENDA OF
## ARAN

## Enda

Prince Enda was a warrior chief,
Who fought for vengeance and for glory.
Victorious he homeward marched
But stayed to tell the stirring story.
Fanchea, his sister, wise and holy,
Listened with sorrow and in shame.
'My grief!' she cried. 'What men lie slain!
What homes destroyed to bring you fame!'

Prince Enda flung away his sword,
Hung up his shield upon the wall.
He said farewell to raid and foray
And, where the cliffs stand grim and tall,
Proud sentinels against the rage
Of ocean storms, on Inis Mor,
Enda, the hermit, vowed he'd live
Alone – in penance, far from war.

But furious pagans, on the heights,
Their weapons seized and all amazed,
While Enda held on high the Cross,
In silence stood, in wonder gazed.
The pagans went, the Christians came,
Scholar and saint to Inis Mor,
Where every rock and every stone
Is holy now, for evermore.

# ENDA OF ARAN

♣

## Prince of Oriel

In the time of Brigid and Patrick, Conall Derg was King of Oriel, the district from Lough Erne to Dundalk. Conall was killed in battle with a neighbouring chieftain, and his son, Enda, swore to avenge his father's death.

Enda called upon the clan and, before Conall's enemies realized that Enda was marching with his men, the young chief had invaded their territory. He was a good leader and his followers were fine fighters, so the raid was victorious.

With Enda at their head they came back chanting the Oriel war song. Their shields were dented and their swords blunt from the stress of battle. The banner bearer limped and the banner which streamed on the wind was tattered. But Enda was too excited to be weary. He was delighted with his success, and so proud that he had returned blow for blow, he forgot the late hour and did not know that every door on the road was barred in fear.

He strode along the bank of the Erne and saw the rising moon reflected in the water, when he remembered that his sister Fanchea's home lay on this road.

Fanchea was a nun and, though younger than her brother, head of the convent. She was praying in her oratory when she heard the shouts of the returning warriors. They stopped a little distance from the door and Enda went forward alone.

'Open!' he cried, beating upon the oaken door with the haft of his spear. 'Open, Fanchea! I have avenged our dead father!'

Fanchea heard the tumult and wondered who came

demanding entrance so late. But she, as well as Enda, had inherited her father's courage and, going alone to the door, she unfastened the bolts and flung it wide open.

To her amazement she found Enda, sword in hand, with shield and helmet, standing there. Beyond, the moonlight glinting on their weapons, his men crowded together, whispering and watching curiously.

'Enda!' cried Fanchea indignantly. 'How can you come to an oratory with weapons in your hands? Aren't you ashamed?'

'Listen,' said Enda, 'I have avenged our father's death and killed his enemies! You should be as pleased as I am.'

'I hoped there would be an end of these raidings and killings when you became chief,' said Fanchea sadly. 'Revenge is an evil thing. Remember they are your own countrymen you have slain.'

'But it's my duty to protect our people,' protested the young man. 'If I didn't I'd be unworthy to be their ruler.'

'Must you go raiding to protect them?' asked Fanchea. 'Are we savages and pagans? You cannot bring our father back. You can make his memory loved and honoured.'

She closed the door slowly and Enda stood there thinking. In their childhood he and Fanchea had been great friends and he had a high opinion of her wisdom.

'Fanchea is right!' he decided. 'I cannot bring back my father. I can only bring misery on others.'

Silently he and his warriors marched away. Now he saw the homes dark and still with terror. He remembered the men who would never return and their friends who would weep for them. Suddenly he was ashamed and sorry for the wrong he had done.

'If only I could be like Fanchea,' he thought.

Before he reached his fort at Rossory, Enda had resolved to give up his possessions and to become a monk.

Fanchea's convent and oratory had no rampart to protect them, but were built openly, the road on one side, the river on the other. Fanchea had no fear, but Enda determined to make her a farewell gift. With the help of his men he raised a high, wide wall of earth all round the settlement, with an entrance so narrow that one or two could defend it against attack.

Bidding good-bye to his sister, Enda journeyed alone to the monastery of Withern, in Galloway, Scotland. This monastery was dedicated to Saint Martin of Tours, the warrior saint, and is sometimes called the House of Martin. From there Enda travelled to Rome. But he had promised Fanchea to return in a year. He kept his word and arrived back at Drogheda.

Enda was glad to be back in his own country, yet he was dissatisfied. He longed for solitude, to be alone with Nature and with God.

Darenia, another of his sisters, was married to Angus, King of Munster, who owned many of the islands in the western sea. Enda asked Angus to give him one of these. The King refused, saying the islands were inhabited by barbarians who would kill him.

'Have as much land as you wish in the Golden Vale,' said Angus. 'Build a monastery there and bring a blessing on us all.'

But Enda implored the King to give him an island, and, because he could not bear to see his friend disappointed, at last Angus agreed.

He gave him Inis Mor, the largest and most westerly of the three Aran islands which lie across the entrance of Galway Bay. So many holy men were buried there, that afterwards Inis Mor was called **Ara** of the Saints.

Enda went up through the west of Ireland until he came
to Galway Bay. Across the stormy water he could see the
three islands – Inis Mor, Inismaan and Inishere – grey
and dim, with high cliffs on the ocean side.

He asked in the fishermen's huts for a boat to take him
across to Inis Mor, but not one man would venture.

'We would be killed,' they told him. 'Stay here, holy
man, and preach to us.'

So Enda travelled farther round the bay. An old fisherman was sorry for him and took the young monk in his
boat to Garomna Island. But he would go no nearer to the
Aran islands.

'I'd sooner try to row out to the Blessed Islands of Hy
Brazil!' he cried. 'The wild waves are kinder than the
savages of Aran. Listen now! I'll tell ye all about them.

'Long ago,' said the old fisherman, 'before you, or I, or
any of the people of our day were dreamed of, the Firbolgs lived in Erin. They were small, dark people, who
dwelt in caves and in the forest. They loved darkness and
hated the light. One day they discovered strangers in the
land: people who were tall and fair, with silk clothes and
light, beautifully made weapons. In a night they had built
cities of white stone with grand houses, high walls and
gates of bronze. The strangers were the Tuatha de
Danann. You've heard tell of them? They were willing to
be friends and offered to divide the country, taking the
open plains and leaving the forests and mountains to the
Firbolgs.'

Enda nodded.

'That was just,' he said.

'I think so,' agreed the fisherman. 'But the Firbolgs

didn't. They attacked the Danann and a great battle was fought on the Plain of Moytura. The Firbolgs were led by their king Mac Erc and the Danann by Nuada.'

'Wasn't he called Nuada of the Silver Hand?' asked Enda. 'Isn't there an old story about him?'

'There is, indeed! Nuada had his hand cut off in battle and one of the Danann, a skilful craftsman, made him a new hand of silver, every bit as good as the old one. Mac Erc was killed and the Danann had the victory. The Firbolgs were given Connaught to live in, while the Dananns took the rest of Erin. In time there was peace between them, but some Firbolgs could not bear to live on the same soil as their enemies and fled to the western islands.'

'And it's those same Firbolgs who're living on Inis Mor?' asked Enda.

'Their children and their children's children and those who came after,' the fisherman told him. 'And I wouldn't go near them for a whole currach-load of fish!'

'I must go!' declared Enda.

All night he sat watching on the shore. He could see fires on the three islands and hear voices chanting strange songs. He prayed and, when the sun came riding over the towering twelve Bens, a long, straight boat came drifting in on the tide.

'That's a queer craft,' muttered the fisherman, who had watched with him. 'Neither skins nor wood have been used in the making of it!'

He helped Enda to pull in the boat. There were no oars, nor a mast, nor sails, and it was shaped the same at both ends. And, although it floated lightly as a currach of skin stretched on a wooden frame, it was made of stone.

Enda stepped into the boat. The tide was against him, yet he was carried out across Galway Bay to Inis Mor.

As he drew in to the island, Enda saw a barren waste of

rocks reaching up to the cliffs which kept back the ocean winds.

Built against the cliffs were walls and, on the highest point a small, dark man, dressed in a skin, stood leaning on a spear.

He did not see Enda in his stone boat for he was gazing southward towards the mountains of Clare.

Enda's stone boat passed the upper end of the island, entered a bay where the water was calm and still, and drifted out again. Enda wished he had an oar or sail for here was surely a good landing place. But, as he prepared to leap ashore, a hidden current swept him on.

He heard the sea thundering in caverns and saw spray shooting up through holes a hundred feet into the air.

Except for the watcher on the wall, the only living things Enda caught sight of were birds. Seals basked on sunny ledges, crabs crawled along the strand and, when he peered over the side of the boat, giant lobsters looked back at him from dark crevices, and the sea swarmed with fish. The watcher seemed the only human creature on the island.

Enda was weary and anxious lest he should be carried away from the islands, when the current turned and tossed the boat into a round bay. A high wave caught the boat and slid it gently on the sandy shore. Enda stepped out and thanked God for bringing him safely. When he raised his head the man with the spear stood a few steps away, watching.

Other armed men were coming down from the fort behind the wall, treading so softly in their pampooties of untanned hide that Enda understood why he had not heard the watcher coming up to him.

'I am a monk and my name is Enda,' he said. 'I wish to

live here and build a monastery. If you are pagans I will make Christians of you all.'

'You cannot stay!' declared the man with the spear. 'Go back to your own country.'

Enda walked about, considering where he should build his cell. A spear whizzed by his head and turning, he saw a man taller and not so dark as the others, standing on a rock, gazing wrathfully at him. The newcomer wore a circlet of gold, set with dull, purple stones, on his shaggy hair, and Enda guessed he was the chief and the one who had flung the spear.

'This is no welcome for a stranger!' said Enda sternly.

'I am Corban, chief of this island,' shouted the man wearing the circlet. 'Here is my stronghold, and I command you to go back where you came from!'

'God brought me here,' replied Enda. 'I came in that stone boat and here I stay! If this island is not big enough for the two of us, 'tis you must go, Corban!'

He cleaned out a dry cavern. Lifting up a long, straight splinter of the grey limestone, Enda fixed it between two rocks. He bound a smaller piece crossways and showed it to Corban.

'Here is the Cross, Corban! While I am on Inis Mor that Cross shall stand. It is the sign of all Christians.'

Corban was angry. He was puzzled too. He could not understand this stranger who came in a stone boat, without oars or sail. He stared to where it lay grounded on a rock, the surf breaking over it, and wondered.

The bravest fisherman, caught in a storm, would not take shelter in this safe anchorage, they so feared the Firbolgs. Yet this young man, unarmed, alone, went about his business and bothered no more about the hostile warriors standing round than if they were sea-gulls.

Corban respected courage, yet that night he sent men to pull down the cross. Enda did not look strong. He had lifted the stone easily, but they could not move it an inch.

Next day the fisherman who had refused to bring Enda to the island rowed over to discover what had happened. He saw the Cross and landed. Other fishermen followed him. They became Christians and helped Enda to build a cell. Almost every day one would come from the mainland to see him, to ask advice and to bring him fish.

Enda lived on fish and seaweed. He drank rain water which he caught in a hollowed stone. By the time he had an oratory built, a boatload of monks sailed to the island. Corban, sulking in his rock fort, saw all this with amazement. He listened to their prayers and hymns and was so impressed by these peaceful invaders, that he decided not only to become a Christian, but to give up the island to Enda and return to Connaught.

When the Firbolgs were gone, Enda and his companions climbed up to the fort which was called Dun Angus.

Inside the wall on which Enda had first seen the watcher, great stones, taller and thicker than a man, were stuck upright in the ground for a space of fifty feet. Then came another rampart twelve feet high. Beyond rose the citadel wall, and on the inner side, platforms were built up where the defenders stood.

Enda and his monks had no need of a fort. They built their monastery on Killeany, or Kill Enda (the Church of Enda) bay, and soon the fame of Enda's sanctity spread throughout Ireland and religious men came to him from every district. Saint Brendan came to Inis Mor and showed Enda where the Islands of the Blest lay, far on the misty horizon. Finnian of Clonard came there, and Finnian of Moville, Saint Colman, Saint Brecan and the great Columcille himself. So many saints found their way to Inis Mor that it was called Ara or Aran of the Saints and its soil was honoured as holy ground.

The Aran islands had seven pagan forts. But from one end of Inis Mor to the other, Enda built churches and oratories. They are ruins now, but the saints are remembered, and if you go to Aran you will find their memory in the names of bays and wells and villages.

# 4

## SAINT BRIGID, THE LIGHT
## OF KILDARE

## Brigid

We see her up the boreen in the twilight,
When the cows come trampling through the gate:
The sods of turf glow and the blue smoke rises
And speckled chickens at the half-door wait.

In through the window where young scholars, bending
Over their books, learn of the wondrous days
When Brigid of Kildare made books like jewels,
Her blue eyes smile, her proud lips murmur praise.

But when the neighbours gather for a ceilidhe
And on the hearth there steams the teapot brown,
And the old, blind fiddler pauses on the threshold,
Saint Brigid enters in with him and sits her down.

# SAINT BRIGID

❧

## *A Chief's Daughter*

WHILE Patrick was travelling up and down the five great roads of Ireland, building a church wherever he stopped, a little girl named Brigid was growing up in her father's dun at Faughart, near Dundalk, above the road to Tara.

Patrick came that way when he was escaping from Melcho, but it was before Brigid's time.

Her mother, Brocessa, was a Christian, so was Brigid. Though Brigid was a chief's daughter, her mother was a slave. The little girl would run from the hall where Dubtach her father and his nobles sat drinking wine and playing chess, to be with her mother in the dairy.

She learned to milk cows and skim the cream, to make butter in a big wooden churn, and while she worked she sang. But she liked listening to stories better than working or singing.

'Tell me a story!' she could coax, the moment she was inside the dairy with her mother.

From the wide doorway they looked down on the road leading from the Gap of the North to Tara.

'Queen Maeve travelled this way,' said Brocessa. 'She was a fine, handsome woman with blazing eyes and long, yellow hair. A great warrior, too, was Queen Maeve!'

'Why did she travel this way?' asked Brigid. 'Did she come from Tara?'

'From farther away than Tara; from the West. She was Queen of Connaught.'

'And why did she come?' demanded Brigid, her elbows

on the table, her eyes following the road as far as she could see.

'She came to invade Ulster because she coveted the Brown Bull of Cooley. There was fighting and killing. The hero Cuchulain was killed and, though Queen Maeve had her way, the Brown Bull fought the White Bull and died, and there was an end of it all.'

'Tell me a story that isn't about killing,' said Brigid.

So Brocessa told her of Patrick, the great Bishop who was going through the country building churches and schools.

'He was a slave, too,' said Brocessa. 'He went along this road on his way to freedom. Now he is the friend of princes, yet he has helped the slaves more than any other man in Erin.'

'I'd love to build churches and go travelling and helping people,' said Brigid.

'So you shall!' declared Brocessa, who thought her daughter the loveliest and cleverest girl in the whole country. 'Learn your embroidery and music and lettering, and be as good as you can. Who knows what is in front of you?'

One day, when Brigid came to the dairy, her mother looked very sorrowful. She told her daughter that a wood-man, in cutting down a tree, had accidentally killed a wolf, a pet wolf, belonging to the King of Leinster.

'The poor wolf,' cried Brigid.

'The poor slave!' sighed Brocessa. 'He has been condemned to death.'

'But he did not mean to kill the wolf!' cried Brigid. 'That's unjust! I must help the man!'

Brigid's father was so fond of her, she could ride in a chariot whenever she wished. So she set off to the King of Leinster's Court. The road passed through a dark wood and, peering out at them from behind a tree, she saw a wolf.

'Come for a ride with me!' she called.

The charioteer had seen the wolf too, and he whipped up the horses, so that they dashed along, the chariot rocking from side to side.

After them came the wolf. Before they were out of the wood he caught up, gave a spring and, when the terrified driver looked back, there was the fierce creature sitting up beside Brigid as peacefully as a dog.

'We ride to save a man's life,' said Brigid.

The wolf put his shaggy head on her knee, and kept it there until they came to the King's dun. Brigid walked up to the entrance, with the wolf trotting at her side. She had put on her new green gown and her golden hair fell over her shoulders to her waist. The guards crossed spears to keep her back, but the wolf lifted his head, looked at them, and at once they let the two companions through.

Brigid went on until she came to where the King sat, turning over the leaves of a manuscript, decorated in gold and bright colours.

'I have brought you a wolf in place of the one that was killed,' said Brigid, bowing as low as she could.

The King closed the manuscript and smiled at her.

'My dear child! My wolf was pure white and could do more tricks than any other creature in Leinster!' he told her.

'Do your tricks!' Brigid ordered the wolf.

The poor animal looked at her in amazement. Suddenly he stood on his hind-legs and, walking up to the King, bowed as he had seen Brigid bow. Then he began to dance and Brigid danced with him.

The King laughed, and from all over the dun people

came running and shouting to one another that a strange girl in green was dancing with a wolf before the King.

'Over and over!' Brigid commanded.

The wolf tucked in his head and turned over and over all round the room. He jumped into the air and twisted round and round before he came down again. As his feet touched the floor, he bowed towards the King.

'That's a wonderful wolf!' cried the King. 'What can I give you for him?'

'A man's life!' replied Brigid.

The King nodded.

'You're a great girl, Brigid! I acted in anger. The slave shall be pardoned!'

Brigid thanked the King and went off.

The wolf looked after her and whined sadly. For three days he moped and fretted. On the fourth she found him sitting outside the dairy when she went to help her mother churn the butter. The King did not ask for him back, and the wolf went everywhere with Brigid and slept at the foot of her couch at night.

She loved all animals and birds, and they loved her. Even the wild geese flying overhead on their way across the ocean would stop their flight when Brigid called them, and drop down to earth.

Brocessa was kind and generous, but Brigid could never refuse anyone what they asked.

She was driving with her father to a neighbouring chieftain's dun. On the way they stopped at another dun and Brigid was left outside in the chariot. She sat watching the people going by and was growing impatient at being kept waiting so long, when a leper came slowly down the road.

Brigid had never seen a leper before and was horrified. When she saw the people draw away from him, she felt only pity for the poor man. He limped along in the dust until he reached the chariot where Brigid sat, and there he stopped.

He did not ask for help. He stood there in silence, his arms folded, his head bent, his few rags caked with mud, looking so wretched and unhappy that tears filled her eyes.

'What can I give him?' she thought. 'I have no money. If only I had put on my necklace, he could have that. But I came out in such a hurry I didn't even bring a cloak.'

She stared at the cushions. They would be useless to a man going the roads. But her father had left his sword, with a jewelled hilt, leaning against the seat.

In those warlike days a sword was very necessary for a Leinster chief and this was the finest Dubtach possessed. He had never before left it out of his sight.

Brigid picked up the sword, though it was so heavy she could scarcely lift it.

'Take this, poor man,' she said. 'You will not have to carry it far. Any warrior or maker of swords will buy it from you.'

Without a word of thanks the leper snatched the sword, thrust it over his shoulder as if it weighed no more than a willow switch and marched away. He no longer walked with his head hanging but held it high. The people, seeing his proud look, and the magnificent sword, made way for him.

Brigid was listening to a ballad singer, though she was still thinking of the leper, when her father returned.

'Now for the chief!' he said, gathering up the reins. 'We should make good speed. The horses have had a long rest. Where's my sword? Surely I didn't come without it!'

Brigid felt anxious.

'I gave it to a leper,' she told him. 'I had nothing else!'

Dubtach stared at her.

'You gave my sword to a leper?' he roared. 'You gave my jewelled sword to a leper? Where is he?'

Brigid pointed up the road.

'He went that way!'

Dubtach slashed the horses. He made them gallop in the centre of the road, so that other chariots had to squeeze by; horsemen were nearly flung from their frightened mounts and foot passengers scrambled up the banks for safety.

There were all kinds of people on the road – chiefs and warriors, fighting men, peasants pushing carts, women carrying bundles and babies, homeless wanderers looking for something to eat and a roof to shelter them. They saw men staggering under goods they hoped to sell before nightfall, but they did not see a leper!

Dubtach shouted to all they met, asking if a leper had passed that way but he did not wait for an answer.

When they came to the crossroads he reined in the horses. He asked and asked of all who went by, but no one had seen a leper with a sword. No one had seen a leper at all!

He turned to Brigid.

'Was there a leper?' he demanded.

'There was!'

Brigid had never told a lie, so her father had to believe her.

'You must be mad!' cried Dubtach. 'Think of giving away my best sword! The sword I won in fair fight from a chief of Munster. I've boasted of its strength and sharpness. A song has been made about its beauty and you give it to a leper!'

'If it had been mine I would have given it,' Brigid told her father. 'It made him forget he was a leper.'

The longer Dubtach thought about it, the worse he felt.

He was still furious when they reached the dun they were bound for. He flung the reins to a guard and strode in. Brigid followed, treading softly so that he would not know she was there.

'If I stay outside I'll be giving away the horses or maybe the chariot!' she thought.

This chief was a Christian. He had heard Patrick preach and he longed for the day when all Ireland would be Christian. He had a great liking for Brigid.

Dubtach was so angry he told what his daughter had done.

'The finest sword you ever set eyes on!' he shouted. 'Twelve jewels in the hilt of it!'

The chief looked at Brigid. She was very downcast and hadn't a word to say for herself.

'If you were outside in the chariot and the leper came to you once more, would you still give him your father's sword?' he asked.

Brigid nodded.

'I would indeed!' she told him. 'You see, I can't help giving. If I'm asked, I must give.'

'I'm a bit that way myself,' said the friendly chief.

He turned to Dubtach.

'Don't blame Brigid. Be proud of her. She is a Christian and Christians should give. I have a sword with fifteen jewels in the hilt. It is not so long, nor so sharp as yours, but if you will forgive her, the sword is yours.'

Dubtach took the sword.

Brigid came home one day to find a stranger in the dairy. Her mother had been sold. Now she understood the terrible wrong of slavery.

'Crying is no use!' she thought. 'What can I do?'

She went to her father and asked him to send her to Brocessa.

'I don't mind being a slave if I'm with my mother,' she told him.

Dubtach was ashamed, but he was too proud to own himself wrong.

'You're a chief's daughter!' he declared. 'Here you stay!'

'I am a slave's daughter, too!' retorted Brigid.

She marched out of the dun and set off in search of her mother.

She walked and walked until she had to sit down by the side of the road.

A fine chariot driven by a young chief came dashing along. Brigid ran out and stood in the middle of the road so that the driver was forced to stop.

'Take me to the boundary!' she ordered.

He had never been so ordered in his life, but he had never met anyone like Brigid before. He obeyed and drove on until they met with another chief in another chariot and he drove with her still further.

It wasn't easy to trace a slave in the Ireland of those days, but at last Brigid came to where her mother was making butter in a dairy as though she had never left Faughart.

Brocessa had been bought by an old Druid and his wife who had become Christians. They had twelve fine cows and they were very proud of these and of their well-built dairy.

Brocessa was skimming the milk, and there was Brigid standing against the sunlight looking in at her.

The poor woman was so happy she cried. She said Brigid must go back to her father at once. Brigid would not go home. She could see her mother was worn out by years of hard work and she stayed to help her.

Soon it was like old times. Brigid made Brocessa sit down while she milked the twelve cows, skimmed the milk, and made little cheeses from sour milk.

A beggar came to ask for a scrap of butter to put on his dry crusts. Brigid gave him a drink of milk as well and one of the little cheeses to carry away with him.

He told the other beggars he met and soon they came to the dairy at every hour of the day. Brigid gave milk, or cheese or butter, to each one of them.

The other slaves told her she would get into trouble when the Druid had visitors and there'd be no milk or butter for the feast.

'There will always be milk, and butter, too!' said Brigid.

The cows had never given such milk. There had never been so much butter or cheese in the place before, and Brigid went on giving.

The Druid liked to present rolls of butter to his friends, because the milk from his cows was very rich. When they came with their baskets to the dairy, Brigid filled them up, and still she gave and gave to the beggars and the poor people who lived in huts near the Druid's home.

The Druid's wife heard Brigid singing as she milked the cows.

'We never had such a dairy before!' she said. 'And such butter! As sweet as if she mixed honey through it. Listen to her singing like a thrush and a blackbird together!'

'She's a good girl,' agreed the Druid. 'Beautiful and clever too. We are old. Why not give her the dairy and the cows with it?'

Brigid would not take their gift. She asked them instead to free her mother and take care of her.

This they promised. Brocessa was given a hut of her own, with a cow and a beehive. She would never have to work hard again.

Brigid settled her mother in the hut, said good-bye and journeyed back to her father's dun. This time she travelled with friends of the Druid, who were taking a manuscript to the High King at Tara.

Dubtach was so glad to have Brigid back again he scarcely grumbled at her for going. Only he didn't leave her in peace for long.

'You're growing up, Brigid,' he said to her. 'Isn't it time you were thinking of getting married?'

Brigid hadn't thought about it at all. She shook her head and sat waiting.

'They say you're very beautiful,' went on Dubtach. 'I'm so used to you I wouldn't know. But there's a young poet and he's here this very day to ask will you marry him.'

He sat back in his chair, feeling very pleased with himself and quite sure Brigid would be as pleased as he was.

In those days a poet was a very grand person. He was next to a chief in rank. Poets were always richly dressed and travelled on the finest horses with many servants following them. For a good poem, a poet might be given a cow, a horse, or even a piece of land. And he was an honoured guest wherever he went.

Brigid could see the young poet sitting his horse in the

gateway of the dun. His crimson robe glittered with gold embroidery, and his black horse was so proud and strong it looked as if made of ebony. Its shoes were of gold, and jewels studded the bridle. The poet's head was thrown back and Brigid knew by his face he was making a poem.

If Brocessa hadn't been a slave and if she hadn't told her daughter of Saint Patrick's wonderful life, Brigid might have thought it grand to marry a poet. But again she shook her head.

'I'm not thinking of marrying,' she told her father. 'Not even a poet!'

'You love poetry!' cried Dubtach, staring at her in amazement. 'Aren't you always and ever learning great, long pieces? That lad has written a poem about Queen Maeve and her masterful ways, and he says you're like her. He has all the old knowledge too. Wasn't he taught by the Chief Druid himself? One day he'll surely be chief poet of Erin! Don't be foolish, Brigid!'

'I won't be foolish,' promised Brigid. 'Only I'll not marry a poet, even to please you. I'll be a nun and build churches. I'll build schools and convents, and help slaves and poor people. They need help!'

'I never heard such nonsense in all my life!' shouted Dubtach. 'You'll marry that poet and be a credit to me!'

'I won't marry a poet!' said Brigid. 'But I will be a credit to you!'

## Under the Oak

Dubtach was a determined man and Brigid was like him. She had, as well, her mother's gentleness and generosity, and she loved learning. Many of the friends of her own age were Christians. When they heard she was determined to become a nun they left their homes and asked Brigid to take them with her.

'First we must find a place where we can live together,' she told them. 'You'll have to work hard and suffer, but you'll be happy, too!'

Some went back home, but seven stayed with her. They carried their own bundles. They had little money and some days they went hungry.

As they trudged along, Brigid told them all she hoped to do. They came to a place where a giant oak stood on a high ridge overlooking the Liffey. The wide branches made a roof from the rain. The great trunk broke the wind. The girls spread out their cloaks and laid down their bundles. Then they looked at Brigid. She was the leader.

'First we must build a shelter!' she told them.

They gathered tall branches, stuck the thick ends in the earth in a circle and bound them together at the top with long, tough grass.

'A fire comes next!' said Brigid.

All around were sticks and branches of fallen trees. While some gathered these, others collected dried leaves for beds. They were beginning on the second hut when two fishermen – an old man and a boy – came climbing up from the river with a basket of freshly caught fish.

'Which is the girl called Brigid?' asked the old fisherman.

'I am Brigid!' And she stepped over to him.

'I should have known,' he said, 'from your golden hair and your friendly eyes. I heard you were going to spend your life helping the people of Ireland, so I'd like to help you. Here's a bit of fish for the dinner and, when you want fish, let out a call for Cathal, the fisherman, or Eamon, his young nephew.'

Cathal emptied out the fish on a patch of grass and back to the river went he and his nephew.

'Who can clean fish?' demanded Brigid.

One girl laughed and answered, 'I can!'

'Now for a good cook and a clear fire,' said Brigid.

The fish was nearly cooked when Brigid saw a man walking along the river bank below. On his back he carried a small, well-filled sack which was powdered with tiny, white crystals – it was a sack of salt.

At once she ran down and stopped him.

'What have you in that sack?' she asked.

He looked at her suspiciously. Salt wasn't easily come by and he had no wish to give even a pinch to a stranger.

'Stones!' he answered jeeringly, and pushed past her.

'Stones let them be!' said Brigid.

At once the weight on his back nearly crushed him.

'I was wrong!' he cried. ' 'Tis salt in the sack.'

'Salt be it!' laughed Brigid.

As she spoke the sack weighed less and the man stood upright.

'Take what you want,' he said.

Brigid plunged one hand in the sack and brought it out full.

'Enough is a feast,' she told him. 'But fish without salt is poor eating!'

By the time the huts were finished the girls had become skilled at building. They made the huts so round and low they looked like beehives. The floor was the earth, with rushes strewn over it. There were no doors but a gap between the branches. Then they set to work on a bigger hut which was to be their chapel.

They built this in the centre and plastered the walls with mud from the river to make them waterproof.

By the time the chapel was ready and Brigid had found a priest who would come to say Mass in it, girls were coming to her from all over the country. Some were the daughters of chiefs, some of slaves. They all had to work. Brigid set each one to the work she could do best. She welcomed those who could sing or play an instrument, copy illuminated manuscripts, or embroider linen for the altar. Not one of them had ever worked so hard or been so happy.

Soon the little community had grown into a big one with skilled workmen to build houses and re-build the chapel so that it was bigger than the oak tree which had once sheltered it.

Dubtach heard of all Brigid was doing and now he was indeed proud of her. He sent her money and horses, and a chariot to travel in.

## Kildare

While huts were being put up to shelter the strangers who were arriving every day, Brigid had a high wall built right round them all. It was made of earth and stones, with sods on top and a heavy wooden gate which could be closed at night.

At Brigid's convent they grew their own food in the fields beyond the high wall. There were workshops, and here skilled craftsmen made ploughs and harrows, rakes and carts. Smiths and carpenters worked there. The corn from the fields was ground at a mill on the river.

The dairies were the finest in Ireland. Brigid's cows were so well kept, their sheds so clean and roomy that their milk was thick with cream, and the nuns in the dairy made butter that was better than any other butter in the country. No wonder she is the patron saint of dairies!

There were houses on the river banks. There were houses in the meadows and the woods. A town was growing up around the convent. Travellers on foot and on horseback were always coming and departing, so Brigid built a guest-house where they could stay. She was known now throughout Ireland for her goodness and generosity, and a road to Cill-dara, 'The Church of the Oak' (now Kildare), was tramped out by the feet of those who came seeking help.

When the food of the settlement and its visitors was secured, Brigid built a library where manuscripts were kept in leather satchels hanging on the walls. Some of her nuns were scholars and she set them to copying manuscripts. Students came asking permission to read in her library. She let them live in her guest-house while they studied, gave them clothes and her blessing when they went away.

When a nun or a student had the gift of colour and of lettering she gave him or her all the pens and brushes and paints that could be used. Kildare became so famous for its illuminated manuscripts that scholars came from all over Europe to see them. *The Book of Kildare* – a copy of the Gospels done in Brigid's school – so glowed with colour on every page that to turn the leaves was like opening a box of jewels.

Girls were always coming to her for help and advice. Some wanted to be nuns; others wanted her friendship. She had time for them all.

One girl came to see the dairy. She was so happy in that wonderful place that it was evening before she dreamed she had been there more than an hour.

'Stay for the night!' said Brigid.

But the girl had to go home to milk the cows, feed the calves and put the hens in their house.

'Leave all that to me!' Brigid told her.

The girl trusted her, stayed all night at the convent and set off home in the morning. The nearer she came, the more anxious she grew.

'I shouldn't have stayed,' she thought, though she was still remembering the happy hours.

She opened the gate. The cows were walking from their shed, mooing contentedly; the calves were ready to jump and butt; when she opened the door of the hen house, the hens cackled sleepily and hopped down from their perches, so well-fed they scarcely bothered to start scratching in the earth.

Brigid had not left the convent for an hour, yet she had kept her word.

Because Brigid was always giving, she expected others to give too. She was planning a monastery for men and Bishop Mel was helping her. As they stood talking of all that was being done in Kildare, across the Curragh came a hundred horses dragging loads of wattles. They belonged to a Leinster chieftain who was building a new house.

'They're just what we want!' cried Brigid, and she sent a messenger to ask for the wattles as a present.

'They are my wattles!' replied the chieftain, Ailell, indignantly. 'And what I have I keep!'

At once the horses stopped pulling their loads and all the shouting and beating could not make them take another step.

Ailell began to laugh.

'Brigid has beaten me!' he said. 'Let her have the wattles!'

Immediately the horses swung round, and off they pranced to where Brigid was planning the new building.

The next day the chieftain sent his most skilled men to help in the work and became one of her great friends.

Indeed, she had friends all over Ireland. She was famous now, and great men came to visit her. Saint Finnian, who loved books, came to see her library of manuscripts. Saint Brendan, the mariner, told her of his voyages and drew charts so that she could understand his wanderings. One of her best friends was Erc of Slane, the poet who had been the first to honour Saint Patrick when he came to King Laoghaire's Court at Tara. He was a very, very old man now.

Brigid loved visitors, and she didn't mind whether they were poor or rich if only they had something interesting to tell her. They were all welcome.

The Seven Bishops of Cabinteely came to Kildare. No one knew they were coming, but they had journeyed a long way and were very hungry. That day more beggars than ever had been to the convent. There was neither milk, butter nor cheese. Every egg had been eaten. Not a scrap of meat, fish, or fowl remained. Even the stale crusts had been given to the wild birds.

'We must have a feast!' declared Brigid. 'It isn't every day seven bishops come to Kildare. Milk the cows!'

'They've been milked twice!' objected the nun in charge of the dairy.

'Milk them a third time!' ordered Brigid. 'They're kind, generous cows, and they'll give their best.'

The cows were milked the third time and gave more than at the two other milkings put together!

She sent other nuns to the fowl houses and back they came with baskets filled with eggs. The cooks found meat and fowl in the larders which had been empty, while the fishermen, Cathal and Eamon, got out their boats and nets again and brought up a boatload of fish. So she made them stay for the feast, and it was such a splendid feast the seven bishops never forgot it.

Brigid always dressed in white, so did the nuns with her. One time Bishop Bran was on his way to Kildare. A mist hid the road, and, instead of seeing lights and fires welcoming them, he and his companions found themselves on a wild, desolate moor. They could see no path. They shouted, but there was no answer. They could not hear even the barking of a dog. The mist grew thicker and they were forced to camp in the darkness without food or fire.

'If Brigid knew, she would never leave us in this plight!' declared Bishop Bran. 'However she did it, she would come to our help!'

The night was bitterly cold. Huddled together for comfort the wanderers fell asleep and every one of them had the same dream –

Through the cold and darkness, a blaze of light shone across the moor. Scrambling up they stumbled towards it and discovered they were at the settlement. The outer gate and the inner gate were wide open, the guest-house shone with fires and torches, and there was Brigid in a white robe, with her friendly smile, coming to welcome them and bring them in. Their bruised feet were bathed with warm water. Then came bowls of hot soup and dishes of meat chopped up with salt and herbs.

The dream lasted all night. In the morning when they woke they saw the road before them. Hurrying on, at the first bend they found Brigid coming in search of them.

She loved music and encouraged all in her convent to

learn singing and to play instruments. One day she called at a fortress in Limerick. The chieftain was away.

'We will wait until his return,' said Brigid. 'It would be bad manners to go before he comes back.'

The room where they sat was very beautiful, with painted walls and embroidered silk hangings. A harp hung on the wall and Brigid's eyes shone when she saw it.

'Who will play while we are waiting?' she asked.

But the chief was the only one in the fortress who could play.

'Take it down!' Brigid ordered the young man who was bringing them sweet mead to drink.

He took down the harp.

'Play it!' commanded Brigid, leaning back in her chair to listen.

'I can't play!' protested the young man.

'Try!' she told him, smiling.

Shaking his head, he ran his fingers over the strings. Suddenly he could play wonderfully.

The others were eager now to try, and one after another every man and woman in the castle played to Brigid and her nuns.

For all her cleverness and generosity there were people who tried to cheat Brigid. One wealthy young man boasted he would play a trick on her. Dressing himself in rags he went to Brigid and begged a sheep. She led the way to her flock and told the young man to choose the sheep he wanted.

An hour later he came back disguised as a very old man leaning on a stick. He stood gazing at her fat, well-coated sheep and sighed.

'Time was when I had sheep as fine as Brigid's. Now I am old and all my sheep have been taken from me!'

'Then take one of mine!' said Brigid.

Again the cheat came, and again, until she had given him seven sheep. He told his friends. Some laughed and thought him a fine fellow. There were others who declared he should be ashamed of himself to cheat anyone as generous as Brigid.

'I only want to show I am cleverer than she is!' chuckled the young man.

He went to his field to admire the seven sheep, but they were gone. Every one of them had returned to Brigid's flock.

About this time two robbers were going through the country stealing where they could. They were on their way to the Liffey valley when they came upon a herd of Brigid's cattle grazing in a field. The boy who should have been guarding them was away searching for a reed to make into a whistle.

The robbers were delighted and drove the cattle out of the field on to the road and down to the river. But not one of the cattle would venture into the water. The robbers pelted them with stones and beat them with switches but the animals would not budge.

At last the two men took off their clothes, tied them to the horns of the cattle and plunged into the river, dragging the animals after them with ropes.

They had reached the middle of the river when the cattle broke free and made for the bank. The robbers swam after them, but the cattle won the race and galloped back home, clothes and all.

Brigid was famous now. The little settlement she and her seven friends had built under the oak was a cathedral city, with convents, churches, monasteries and colleges. All over Europe learned men admired the work she had done.

Like Saint Patrick she loved travelling to every corner of Ireland. She travelled in a chariot drawn by two horses. A driver sat on the small seat in front and two nuns sat inside with her.

She did not always keep to the main roads but followed mountain paths, crossed bogs and journeyed through the forests. Every place she stayed in was called after her. She rescued slaves and captives, and made peace between warring chieftains. Her convent was a sanctuary for all who were hunted, human beings or animals.

Sometimes she is called Mary of the Gael, for she had a great love for Mary, the Mother of Christ, and, in a wonderful dream, she was with the Holy Family in their flight from Egypt, sharing their perils and their faith.

In her own lifetime she was honoured as a saint. The great oak which had sheltered her was held sacred for five hundred years, and through all the wars and fighting of that time, no one dared draw a sword or hurl a spear in its shade.

And, when she died, a great flame was lit upon her tomb and was kept burning for a thousand years.

# 5

# BRENDAN
# THE VOYAGER

## Brendan

Brendan, the sailor, sailed into the sunset,
Into the clouds where sea meets the sky:
Turrets of silver and rooftops of jasper,
Stairways of azure and domes set on high.

    Into the west he sailed,
    To the ocean's rim;
    Until earth's winds failed
    And stars grew dim.

Behind lie the strand and the white, scattered cabins;
The mountains sink down and the friendly lights fade;
The stars they are distant and mists hide the moonlight;
Endless the waves toss – now silver, now jade.

    Onward he sailed and on.
    No sleep, no rest.
    Others have sought, he found
    The Isles of the Blest.

# BRENDAN THE VOYAGER

♣

## A Traveller's Story

BRENDAN was born where Kerry looks out upon the Atlantic, where the sun is hot upon the rocks one moment and the next they are hidden by a creeping white mist.

He played among these rocks and went down with the other children to greet the fishing boats pulling in with their gleaming cargoes. He learned to watch for signs of changing weather and see great distances. In the winter, when the fisherwomen shut out the storms and the neighbours sat around the fire telling stories and wonders, he listened until he fell asleep.

The stories he liked best were about islands, especially the Blessed Islands of Hy Brazil. He made up his mind that as soon as he possibly could he would go in search of the wonderful islands he heard about.

Instead of seeking islands he went to a school kept by Saint Ita of Munster, then to study under Saint Erc, who ordained him a priest.

It seemed that Brendan had forgotten his early ambition to sail in search of the islands the Kerry people talked about. He lived in Ardfert for a while and then built a cell at the foot of Brandon Hill.

Now he was among the Kerry fishing folk again and watched their boats sailing out before dawn and coming back in the twilight. Sometimes he went with them.

He climbed Brandon Hill so that he could see farther out across the ocean, and decided to stay there. He was clever at building cells, but he was beginning to think he would sooner be building boats.

One evening he was sitting on the stone seat outside his

cell, feeding his pet crow, when a man came climbing the narrow track.

'Here's someone who needs supper and a lodging for the night,' Brendan told the bird, hurrying in to blow up the fire and set a cauldron of soup to heat.

He was cutting a pollock in slices, when the traveller stopped outside, sat down on the stone seat and sighed loudly.

'You're welcome!' said Brendan, going out to him. 'There's not many come up here. 'Tis a long climb and leads nowhere at all.'

'I thought I'd be able to see the islands, but my eyes are growing dim,' said the stranger sorrowfully.

'Come to supper now!' and Brendan led the way.

Brendan had rolled a big, flat stone inside his cell to serve as a table. He sat on a log of wood and gave the only chair to his guest. Both were hungry and spooned their soup in silence. Then Brendan began to toast the slices of pollock.

'There's no fish I like less than pollock!' he grumbled. 'If I'd known you were coming I'd have had a cut of salmon, or maybe a lobster. But the crow there has a strange liking for pollock.'

'Pollock, or salmon, or lobster, 'tis all one!' declared the traveller.

Brendan was sorry for his mournful guest. He was long and thin and kept his cloak wrapped round him the whole time. His dim eyes looked out of the door as though seeking something and, even when he spoke to Brendan, he did not look at him.

Brendan poured out two cups of mead and took down a basket of flat, sweet cakes, with roasted nuts in them, from the shelf where he kept his provisions.

'You'll not drink better mead nor eat sweeter cakes if

you travel the whole kingdom of Kerry!' he declared. 'Old Nanno made them both and there's not her equal for them.'

The stranger did not answer and Brendan feared he had as little interest in mead and cakes as in fish.

Suddenly he leaned forward and pointed.

'The Islands!' he cried. 'There are the Islands! I knew I should see them. I knew!'

'Those are only clouds!' said Brendan. 'They always come at sunset. There is one like a silver mountain. Sometimes they are like the ghosts of islands. But in the morning they are gone. I used to watch out for them when I was a child. Nanno, the woman I lived with down in the village, used to tell me wonderful stories about them, and I dreamed that when I was a man I would sail out to them. Now I am wiser. I know they are only clouds!'

And he sighed as deeply as his guest.

'You were wiser as a child!' declared the stranger. 'They are islands. I have been there, Brendan. Do what you dreamed of! Set out upon the ocean and you shall see beauty you never imagined. Some say one of those islands is Paradise!'

Brendan listened in wonder. He felt he was a child again.

'Tell me more!' he said. 'Tell me more!'

He listened until his companion's voice was hoarse and tired. He was ashamed of himself.

'You need rest,' he exclaimed, 'and I have kept you talking. Lie down and sleep. Tomorrow we shall make great plans.'

The traveller stretched himself on Brendan's bed. The sun set over the ocean, and islands, more and more islands, came swimming up over the horizon. Were they islands, or only clouds? Brendan stared until his eyes ached. Darkness came. He sat on his stone seat, the crow on his shoulder, and fell asleep.

He woke before dawn. The crow was stalking up and down, flapping her wings and cawing to waken him.

He glanced seaward.

'Clouds still there!' he told the crow.

The bird fluttered up to his shoulder and perched there, quiet now.

There was the silver mountain, half-hidden by mist. The others were farther away, but surely he could see trees and, on the wind which blew shoreward, came the singing of birds.

The traveller stepped out into the chill morning air.

'Do you still think they are clouds?' he asked.

Brendan looked at him with troubled eyes.

'I have lived many years on this coast,' he said. 'Fishermen are sailing out every day, yet never have I heard of islands over yonder, where we see them now.'

The stranger smiled.

'Have you never heard tell of islands that are there for some and not for others? Of islands that look near when they are far away, and look distant when they are near?'

'I have, indeed!' said Brendan. 'There are legends, too, of Hy Brazil, the Isles of the Blest.'

'I have been there!' the traveller told him. 'Did you never hear of Mernoke?'

Brendan thought. Surely he had heard the name of Mernoke, long ago.

'I heard of Mernoke,' he said slowly. 'He set sail for Hy Brazil, but he never came back! Old Nanno saw him go. She did not see him return.'

The traveller gazed out at the islands.

'I am Mernoke!' he declared. 'I have returned. Go,

Brendan! See what I have seen. See all you can of the world while you are in it!'

Still Brendan hesitated. The cloud islands were so lovely he hated to look away from them and still he feared they were only clouds.

'They are worth the journey,' Mernoke urged him. 'How I wish I could go with you!'

'We shall go together!' said Brendan. 'Mernoke, you have made me believe!'

Brendan gazed once more over the ocean. When he turned again the stranger was gone.

## To the Islands

'Time we were on our way!' said Brendan to the crow.

The bird strutted off down the path, stopping and blinking back at him every few yards. Brendan gathered up his few belongings, rolled them into a bundle and went after the crow.

He was so happy he sang, and when he came down to where the men were tarring their boats and an old woman was making a net, they stopped working, pleased to see him among them.

The children were paddling in the pools left by the tide, but they came splashing in to see what Brendan wanted.

' 'Tis a long time since ye were with us, Brendan,' said Nanno, the old woman whose cabin had been a second home to him when he was a child.

'I'm thinking of taking a boat out to the islands,' Brendan told her.

'To the islands!' cried the old woman.

'To the islands!' repeated the fishermen, crowding round Brendan.

'I have seen Mernoke,' Brendan told them. 'He has returned.'

'Ye were always wanting to be off seeking the islands,' said Nanno, laying down the net. 'But the islands are a long way. Better stay in Kerry and build churches, Brendan. We sorely need them.'

'I'll come back and build all the churches I can,' promised Brendan. 'But now I have seen Mernoke I know I must journey to the islands. They may not be very far. Look! You can easily see them now!'

The old woman strained her eyes and the fishermen looked their hardest.

'Sure, that's only clouds ye're after seeing, Brendan avic,' the old woman told him.

'Didn't I often hear it said, and in your house too, they may be clouds to some, but they are the Isles of the Blest to others?' asked Brendan.

'Ye did, indeed,' said Nanno, thoughtfully. 'And why wouldn't ye be the one to find them real islands, for ye're a very holy young man, Brendan.'

'Don't go!' cried one of the fishermen. 'Don't go! 'Tis only a story we tell around the fire in winter, during the long dark nights. I remember a lad who believed in that story and he set off without telling a soul, to find them self-same islands. He never came back, but the tide brought in his boat, and it empty. Don't go!'

'I must go!' said Brendan. 'Mernoke came back. Why shouldn't I? The sea is God's as well as the earth. I am not afraid!'

'Ye can't go today,' Nanno told him. 'Ye must have a boat and a good one. And ye can't go alone!'

'Who will lend me a boat?' asked Brendan.

The fisherman who had spoken nodded towards a large currach turned upside down among the rocks.

'There's the boat the other poor fellow took to go seeking islands,' he said. 'No one will grudge ye that. We'll overhaul it and, as far as boats go, ye shall have the best. It shan't be said that Kerry people didn't stand by their own.'

'Then there's food for the voyage,' the old woman reminded them.

'Time enough!' said Brendan. 'Time enough!'

He was good with boats. He and the fisherman examined the empty currach and made sure that the wooden frame was sound and the hide covering untorn.

He decided to wait until the next day, and that night there was a great gathering in Nanno's cabin to wish him Godspeed. Everyone who came brought something for the voyage.

Brendan was out early the next morning for he had been too excited to sleep. As he and his friends were loading the currach he saw a group of young monks coming along the shore road. Toiling after them was an old monk. They all carried bundles and when they saw Brendan standing there, they raised a shout – 'Brendan! Brendan! Wait for us!'

When they knew Brendan had seen them they waited till the old monk caught up, for he was their leader.

'We heard you were going to seek for the Islands of the Blest so we left our cells to come with you,' he explained. 'These young fellows can row and fix a sail. They can fish and do any work you need. And they bring food for the voyage. Here is dried meat and a bag of flour. This is meal, and these are cups and spoons and a saucepan to boil our food. I am old and my burden is a harp. When you are sad my music will cheer you and, let me tell you, Brendan, there may come a time when music will mean more to you than drink or food!'

'There never was a time when I didn't love music,' said Brendan. 'You and your harp are very welcome. All of you are welcome, and I'm thankful for the provisions. We'll start out now with the fishing fleet.'

They set to work stowing away the bundles they had brought.

'Will there be space for us all?' asked Brendan, for the boat seemed already loaded.

They rushed to board the currach, for no one wanted to be left behind. But the crow was first. With a loud 'Caw! Caw!' it fluttered to the prow of the boat and clung there, its wings outspread.

'Let ye leave that dismal creathure behind, Brendan!' called old Nanno. ''Tis no sort of a figurehead for yer boat. I'll care for it till ye come back.'

'My crow has lived with me so long, we'd be lonely away from one another,' declared Brendan as he leaped after the others.

Nanno was still grumbling when the oars dipped into the water, and away from the boat slip went Brendan's currach, leading the fishing fleet. The sun shone out of the eastern sky in such glory that the boats, the men, and even the crow now sitting on Brendan's shoulder, and the sea-gulls swooping over them, seemed made of gold.

'Farewell!' called Brendan.

He rubbed his eyes. The boat slip, the cabins, the strand, the fishing fleet he had thought so close behind, were hidden in a thick white mist. Yet his boat was in sunshine and, when they put up a sail, it swelled in the wind, so that the rowers could pull in their oars and rest.

'Play a tune that will reach the ears of those watching on the shore,' said Brendan to the harper.

The old monk obeyed. He played until they forgot time, and night had fallen before they remembered they were hungry and sleepy. The fishermen in their boats drew in their nets again and again until the boats could hold no more. Then they turned shorewards without a sail being raised or an oar dipped, while the old woman and those who stayed with her were lost in happiness.

## Among the Islands

The next day the monks took it in turn to watch lest they should pass the islands without seeing them. Brendan took the first watch, standing up, his arm about the mast, while he listened as his companions told where they were born, how they became monks, and all their wanderings and adventures.

'Land!' he cried. 'Straight ahead!'

A great white cliff rose before them, straight up from the water's edge. The steersman turned the boat's head so that they kept at a fathom's distance from the shore. They all sat silent, wondering what lay beyond the cliff which extended as far as they could see, with great waves leaping against it.

On they sailed.

'This cannot be an island!' declared one. 'It is too large. Surely we have crossed the ocean and reached an unknown land.'

'Not so large as you might think,' said Brendan. 'Ask the steersman!'

' 'Tis an island, sure enough. We've been round it once and now we're going round again.'

'Where's the sense in going round and round?' demanded the monk who had charge of the provisions. 'It's a great rock where only a bird could land. Aren't we foolish to be wasting our time and our food?'

'An island is an island!' Brendan told them. 'And isn't it islands we're seeking? Who knows what wonders may lie beyond that high cliff.'

'And haven't we all the time there is?' asked the harper.

So they sailed round the island again and night came on.

For three days they went round and round. The sea was smooth, the wind so light they had to use the oars, yet the great waves leapt higher and higher against the cliff.

At last Brendan decided to abandon the island.

'Before sunset we'll surely come upon another,' said the harper, trying to comfort him.

As he spoke Brendan cried out –

'There's a harbour, and a safe one! See! When the waves drop! Out oars and make a dash for it!'

The steersman turned the currach. The oars dipped into the water and they made straight for the cliff. Only Brendan could see the opening, but his companions trusted him. Into that turmoil of foam they sped and there – a narrow channel, with scarcely room for their oars, opened out into a perfectly round harbour.

The cliff was like a wall about the island. They saw flowers and fruit trees, grass-grown paths and steps leading down to the harbour. Among the trees rose a white building with turrets which glittered in the sun. But they could see no inhabitants, not even an animal or a bird. The only sounds were the waves beating against the cliff outside and a faint breeze rustling the leaves.

They rowed in to the steps and jumped on shore. Even Brendan was glad to feel solid earth under his feet. He fastened the currach, then set off along a path which seemed to lead to the hall. It wound in and out among the trees, so that when they expected to arrive at the door they were as far from it as ever.

'If we can't enter, we'll help ourselves to the fruit,' said Brendan. 'Wouldn't it be a pity to waste it!'

No two trees bore the same kind of fruit and the monks, who were very tired of dried meat and uncooked porridge, rambled about, eating the fruit and admiring the flowers.

Brendan came out from under a tree with a sweet, yellow fruit like an enormous plum in his hand, when he saw that they had reached the hall.

A broad belt of closely-cut grass surrounded it and the door stood open a little way.

Keeping close together the monks walked across the grass and stood in the doorway.

A thick chain of gold hung down and Brendan tugged it. Instead of a bell ringing they heard a trumpet which deafened them.

'If there's anyone in the place, that should bring them out!' he said.

The noise ceased, and still no one came.

'Come along,' said Brendan. 'We'll have a look at the place!'

He pushed the door wide and went in, the others crowding after.

A round table stood in the centre of the hall. It was loaded with silver cups and bowls, beautifully chased, and all down the walls hung golden bridles.

'I'd love to see the horses who'd wear those bridles,' said Brendan. 'They must surely belong to a prince!'

'But where are the horses and where is the prince?' asked the harper. 'Will I play a tune?'

'No!' replied Brendan. 'Let the silence of this great hall be unbroken.'

They all trooped out and he pulled the door behind them.

Back they went through the trees, not troubling to follow a path and, though the lovely fruit hung within their reach, not one of them put out a hand to pluck it.

The monks stepped into their currach, pulled across the harbour, to the narrow passage and out through the leaping waves. When they looked back not even Brendan could see the entrance.

They put up the sail and soon the cliff island was no bigger in the water than a sea-gull. Brendan sat wondering about that strange island, and one of the monks put it into a song which he sang while the harper played.

As his fingers plucked the strings, other singers joined in and the monks realized that unseen birds were singing to them.

The youngest monk of all was watching.

'There are trees growing up out of the water,' he said. 'The branches are crowded with birds of all colours. They look like flowers but they are singing to welcome us.'

Now the others could see this island of birds and trees. The birds were small and did not stay still for a moment, but hopped from branch to branch, changing places with one another, fluttering their wings but not flying, and singing the whole time. They were so gay and friendly that the monks rowed in under the trees to watch and listen.

As suddenly as they had heard the singing, so it ceased, and the monks sat looking at an island of trees whose leaves were pink and red, blue and yellow, scarlet and green.

They were eating dried meat and wishing they had brought some fruit from the Island of the Golden Bridles, when the boat was seized by a current and sped through the water so that a wave was thrown up on each side high enough to sink them.

'Keep still and pray!' advised Brendan. 'God has brought us safely this far. Why should we be afraid?'

The boat began to go round and round, while the water formed a high circular wall which rose higher and higher as they plunged down. They were caught in a gigantic whirlpool and wondered if they would ever come out of it.

Yet they sat still and prayed their hardest.

To their delight the boat began to ascend, spinning round and round until they were giddy. Soon they were tossed out on the surface of the sea, and they rowed as they had never rowed before to escape from the whirlpool.

On each side they saw water flung into the air, then falling back with a crash which shook the boat, but they rowed steadily.

Brendan did not look back, though the others peered over their shoulders to see the dangers they had left behind, so he was the first to catch sight of a beautiful girl drifting along in the water. Her fair hair covered her like a golden cloak and Brendan was horrified to see a spear thrust through her body. The girl's eyes were closed and her face was white and still.

When he cried out the other monks saw her.

'The poor, lovely girl!' exclaimed the singer.

'She is a mermaid,' declared the harper. 'No human girl has a fish's tail!'

Brendan saw she was indeed a mermaid.

'How can I help her?' he wondered.

They stopped the boat and pulled her to the side. As gently as he could, Brendan drew out the spear and the mermaid opened her sea-green eyes.

'Who are you?' she asked. 'You look kind, not like those pirates who killed me.'

Brendan told her who they were and the reason of their journey.

'You can live now as a mermaid,' he said. 'In the end you will become foam on the waves. Or I can baptize you and send you straight to heaven.'

'I will go to heaven,' she said. 'Baptize me now and let me go, for I have suffered too much in this world.'

Brendan baptized her and, as he spoke the last words, the mermaid closed her eyes and sank down beneath the waves.

But they saw her golden hair still shining through the water and not one of them spoke for several hours.

## The Moving Island

Since they left Kerry, Brendan had kept an account of the time and he knew that Easter was drawing near.

'I'd like to celebrate Easter on land,' he said to his followers. 'Wouldn't it be a great pity if, among all the islands of the sea, we couldn't find a small one when we need it most.'

'Isn't that an island of a sort?' asked the harper, who could see farther than any of them, though he was the oldest.

Brendan looked. They all looked but they could see nothing, only green water tipped with white. When they mounted the swell of the rolling waves, there was a green valley below and, when they descended, a smooth, green hill rose above them. There were birds in the air and fishes in the sea but, on the surface, they couldn't see even a streamer of seaweed.

'Follow the line of my finger, where I'm pointing!' said the harper.

A patch appeared on the water. The waves rose round it, foam tossed across, but there it remained, the barest island they had seen.

There were no trees, no grass or flowers, but to the monks, weary of being crowded in a small boat, it was very welcome. There would be room to walk about and stretch their legs, and they could change places without taking care.

Even the pet crow, who had been very good and patient all through their wanderings, was tired of the continual motion. She gave a joyous caw, fluttered into the air and was the first on the island.

Brendan lit the Paschal fire and said Mass.

For most of them it was their first Easter away from Ireland. The strangeness of their surroundings made the Mass more friendly and beautiful than ever.

As the fire died down the island quivered. The old harper was flung full length and, when they helped him to his feet, he clutched Brendan.

'This is no island! Let us get away before we are dragged to the bottom of the sea!'

Again the island trembled and they hurriedly got into their boat. As Brendan, the last to leave, stepped on board, the island plunged down, then rose high above them. They saw a great fish's head at one end, a tail at the other, and the force of its plunging nearly swamped the currach.

The monster's red eyes glared at them. They hoisted the sail and put out the oars as well.

' 'Twas asleep, no doubt, and the heat of the fire roused it,' declared the harper. 'We should be thankful we're saved!'

On they journeyed, coming to islands they had never heard of, yet never finding those Mernoke had discovered.

'I would like to meet him again!' said Brendan. 'We'd have some grand tales to tell one another.'

They awoke one morning and saw a great shining column which soared into the sky so that they could not see the summit. As they gazed, a tablet of stone came hurtling down to them. It floated on the sea and when Brendan picked it up, he read engraved on it –

'This is not the island ye seek.'

They rowed on without attempting to land.

Their provisions were finished and the ocean looked empty. The monks' clothes were worn. They no longer talked and laughed but sat silent, dreaming of their own places. Even the crow drooped, and Brendan, looking around the currach, realized that he was near the end of this voyage.

'I wonder,' said Brendan, 'would it not be wise to turn homeward?'

Not one answered. But he read his answer in their eyes.

Brendan could have kept on and on, but he knew the others were longing to return to the work they had left. There had been no quarrels, no grumblings in spite of all the hardships and dangers they had been through, yet not one of them shared his great love of islands.

They sailed homeward and, when they saw the blue mountains of Kerry rising up from the sea, Brendan thought he had never seen a more beautiful place.

The shore was crowded. For all over Munster people had come to welcome them. When the battered currach was seen, skimming the waves, a great shout went up and the fishermen rushed into the water to carry the wanderers, currach and all, on their shoulders.

'How did you know we were returning?' asked Brendan.

'Ah, we just thought 'twas time you were home,' replied old Nanno. 'And I had a dream!'

## The Second Voyage

Now that Brendan was home again he worked harder than ever and he didn't stay in one place. He went to Thomond and founded a monastery at Inis da Druin. Then he went to Wales and Scotland, and visited monasteries in Britain. After three years he came back to Ireland.

Through all his teaching and preaching he kept thinking of islands. There must be so many he hadn't seen.

He visited Saint Ita, who had taught him, and told her that he wanted to go on another voyage. Saint Ita didn't approve of long voyages in currachs. She advised Brendan to build a large, wooden ship with a fixed mast and, knowing her wisdom, he began to have trees cut down at once.

When it was told that Brendan was going on another voyage, monks and students from all over Ireland went on a pilgrimage to ask him to take them.

As soon as the ship was ready, a stream of carts and horses crossed the mountains into Kerry. Everyone who had heard of the first voyage longed to go. Brendan had to choose his companions very carefully, and all those who couldn't go were determined to help.

Sacks of grain, boxes of fruit and spices, dried and salted fish, meat, meal, and bundles of herbs were piled along the strand.

Some sent clothes and sandals, manuscripts for the

travellers to read and candles to give them light. There was so much they could have loaded the ship three times over. Brendan gave what was left to the poor and, for a whole year, there was no poverty in Kerry.

It was the finest ship Brendan had ever seen. He was proud of it and of the men who had built it. As they pushed away from the shore, he felt sorry for those left behind.

'Yet I suppose they pity us,' he thought.

The voyagers saw the lights long after the cabins and people had disappeared in the darkness. Brendan steered the ship. He had no compass. In those days they did not know the world was round. But at night they had the stars, by day the sun, and Brendan was one of the most wonderful navigators who ever lived.

He remembered the Island of the Golden Bridles and wondered would they still be there. Would he see the horses they were made for and the men who rode them? Or would the island still be deserted, with its great hall and its many fruit trees?

The ship came to where that island had been. But there was only the ocean and not a sight of land. This puzzled Brendan. He sailed on and was thinking he had been foolish to bring so many with him when the man in the bow cried out that there was land in sight.

They drew towards an island with a rocky shore. Inland were green meadows. The ship's company were thinking how pleasant it would be to walk through grass under trees, when they saw that on every rock stood a dwarf holding a stone, ready to cast it at the ship when it came near enough.

'We are friends!' cried Brendan. 'We seek the Isles of the Blest and we'll do no harm!'

The dwarfs howled and made faces at them.

'We'll anchor here,' said Brendan. 'When they under-stand we really are friendly, they will want us to land.'

He called out that he had presents for all on the island.

One of the dwarfs hurled a large stone. It fell short and only tossed up a shower of spray.

'We are Christians!' cried Brendan. 'If you will listen you shall hear all about Christ and the Kingdom of God!'

The dwarfs would not listen. They set guards all round the island, and never by day or night did they leave the shore unguarded.

For seven days and nights Brendan and his companions remained there. They could not sleep because of the ter-rible noise made by the dwarfs, and on the eighth day they decided to depart.

'Haul in the anchor!' commanded Brendan.

Two men tugged at the chain but the anchor would not budge. Two more went to help them and they were no better. Then all who could find holding space pulled and hauled. Still the anchor held firm.

' 'Tis stuck between two rocks!' declared Brendan. 'Leave it there!'

Off they went without an anchor, thankful to sail out of reach of the dwarfs' threats and howls.

## The Island of Judas

Now they sailed north. The days became shorter, the nights longer, and all the time they were very cold. The sea was grey and blocks of ice swept by. There was sleet on the wind which moaned in the rigging, and some of the voyagers were afraid. They began to wonder would they ever see Ireland again.

'It was a good, pleasant place to be living in,' sighed one. 'Why did we leave it?'

'Kerry is not the only place in the world,' said his friend, trying to comfort him. 'Brendan is right to see all he can. The whole world will envy us if he brings us to the Isles of the Blest.'

As he spoke they saw the iceberg – a mountain of ice – blue and cold. They crowded on all the sail the ship would carry, for a strong current was bearing them closer and closer.

'Is that a man?' cried Brendan. 'We must rescue the poor unfortunate. Quick, or he'll be perished with cold!'

So they let the current take them in until, by leaning outward, they could touch the towering wall of ice.

The man lay stretched on a sheepskin rug. His hair was long and matted, his face thin, his eyes wild and unhappy.

'We'll throw a rope! Are you strong enough to catch it?' shouted Brendan.

The man lay staring at them without moving.

Brendan began to tie the rope about his own body.

'Be ready to pull us on board!' he said. 'I'll have to carry the poor fellow!'

When the man saw that Brendan was attempting to rescue him he jumped up and ran to the water's edge.

'Keep back!' he said. 'You cannot help me! But God reward you for your pity! I am Judas who betrayed Our Lord.'

A groan of horror went up from everyone on the ship, everyone except Brendan.

'Why are you here?' he asked.

'Because God, too, has pity, even for Judas. Every good act I did in my life helps me now. Once I went by a road that had a great hole in it. I was young and strong. I could leap across. But an old woman was on the road and I filled the hole so that she could keep on her journey. The stones are here to keep the chill of the ice from me. I gave my coat to a leper when he shivered in a storm. Here is the sheepskin to give me a soft bed. But nothing can cure the misery in my own heart. Pray for me, Brendan!'

'I will!' promised Brendan with tears in his eyes.

When he wiped away the tears the iceberg had disappeared and the ship sped on to the north.

'It grows colder every day!' grumbled the sailors. 'Where's the sense in sailing up to the dark, cold north when we might be warming our bones in the sunny south?'

Brendan was sorry for them, so he tried to turn the ship. He could not, for it would go in no direction but the north.

'Island ahead!' sang out the watch.

As they came nearer they saw an island of green and purple rocks. When the sun shone it looked a garden of grass and flowers. When clouds hid the sun Brendan thought he had never seen so desolate a place.

'There's surely no human being living here!' grumbled the sailors.

Brendan could never pass by an island, so they put out the oars, and, rowing swiftly, flung a rope over a round rock, for they had left their anchor at the Island of Dwarfs, and made the ship fast.

There wasn't a harbour, only a crack between the rocks where a small boat might squeeze through.

Brendan lifted out the smallest currach they had on board. Thrusting it into the crack, he swung himself down to it. He had no need of oars but pressing his hands against the sides of the cliff, which rose far above his head, he forced the currach into a pool near the centre of the island.

At the entrance to a cave above the pool stood an old man with a long, white beard and shaggy hair. His only garment was a goatskin. Bending down, he pulled the currach along to a flight of stone steps which led from the water and helped Brendan to step on shore.

'Welcome!' he said. 'It is long since I saw one of my own kind, but I am glad to see you here.'

He led the way into his cave.

A fire of driftwood burned on a stone hearth at the entrance and a fish, stuck on a splinter of rock, was sizzling over the glowing wood.

'I haven't had a bit of fresh fish since I left Kerry!' declared Brendan, as he and the old man sat side by side before the fire. 'I have the cleverest crew that ever sailed a ship on the ocean but I never noticed a good fisherman among them.'

'I have fresh fish twice a week,' the hermit told him.

'Is the fishing good here?' asked Brendan.

The hermit shook his head.

'I wouldn't know. I have a friend who feeds me, and feeds me well. There he comes!'

A seal's smooth, shining head was thrust up through the water by the steps. In its mouth the creature held a long, spotted fish. The seal laid it down, rolled up beside it, lying there, looking at the hermit with friendly eyes and grunting gently.

The hermit went down the steps and picked up the fish. He stroked the seal's head before he returned.

'I'd be lonely without my friend,' he said. 'When I came here first, I didn't know how to manage at all. My boat was wrecked in a storm and I was flung up here, bruised and senseless. The seal brought me a flint and showed me a pile of driftwood. When I had a fire burning he went fishing and caught me a fine mackerel. Twice a week he comes, and I think he understands when I talk to him.'

Brendan was sorry to leave the hermit and his seal, but he knew there were other islands in the ocean.

## Other Islands

Brendan was still talking to the monks about the hermit and his seal when the sun went down. They had sailed into summer and, in these northern latitudes, the night was short. This night a thick mist was rising which hid the sky and even the waves from them. They had to grope about the ship and the frightened sailors huddled together, talking of their homes in low voices.

Suddenly a red glow appeared in the sky.

'That's not the moon!' said Brendan, 'and it couldn't be the sun.'

'I don't like the look of it!' murmured the monk standing beside him. 'It's a great smoking fire!'

For days the sea had been very silent. Now a clanging and hammering filled the air with tumult. The ship was approaching the fire, and those who could see farthest said there were forges all along a mountainous shore, with giant smiths working at them.

'Be ready with the oars!' ordered Brendan. 'We may need them to escape.'

Beyond the forges and their grimy workers a cave opened into the side of the mountain and flames came from it. As they stared, a shaggy, hideous form, dressed in burning rags, dashed out and hurled a glowing mass of metal at the ship with a mighty pincers.

Luckily it fell short but went into the water with such a

splash that everyone on deck was drenched. The heat was so great that the water boiled and dense clouds of steam hid them from the shore. Every oar was thrust out and the wind swelled the sail. But, as they departed, more burning masses were flung after them.

In the hurry and excitement the voyagers did not realize that they were sailing southward until they saw a clear sky and the rising moon.

That night they came to an island that was like a great block of chalk, white and gleaming. Big, square houses were built back from the shore. They went into each house in turn and found them all empty, except the last, which was the largest.

When they entered this they found four stone pillars set in the middle of a lofty hall. A small white cat was leaping from one pillar to the other. When Brendan and his companions came in, it looked at them without fear but would not stop leaping. Brendan thought he would like to take it home with him but the cat leapt so swiftly he could not catch it. As he went out of the hall, he looked back and the cat was still jumping on the four pillars.

Another day they came to a small island which was divided in two by a bronze fence. On one side was a flock of black sheep and on the other the sheep were all white. A tall shepherd was tending the flocks and Brendan saw him put a white sheep among the black. Its fleece turned black at once. He put a black sheep among the white, when it immediately turned white like those around it. The sailors were so terrified that, out of pity for them, Brendan sailed on without landing.

'Maybe it's as well we should return,' said Brendan. 'But there is so much of the world I haven't set eyes on.'

As he spoke, before him rose the rocky coast of Kerry. There was Nanno's cabin. It had been freshly thatched with oaten straw and the walls had been whitened. It glittered clean and bright as if made of gold and silver. Brendan was happy again.

'To come home to such beauty is real happiness!' he thought.

Though he had returned home a second time, Brendan was still a wanderer. He travelled across Ireland to visit Iona, the island of Columcille. From there he preached all through the islands of the Hebrides. Some of the old Scottish songs tell of Brendan, and his strange journeys. He went to Britain and, on his way back, came to Loch Corrib and saw the islands scattered there. On one of the loveliest – Inchiquin – he built a monastery. His nephew, Moinenn, helped him. They dug out the stones, carried them on their backs, built the cells and the little oratory.

His sister, Saint Briga, followed him from Kerry, for they loved one another dearly, and he built her the convent of Annaghdown on the shore of the lake. His greatest work was the founding of the monastery of Clonfert, by the Shannon. At one time there were three thousand monks and scholars there, and many holy and distinguished men were educated at Clonfert.

Still he wandered, going over to Brittany, where he saw the pagan ruins at Aleth and at Carnac, the Place of Cairns. Here, there were great stones, like those of the Druid altars in Ireland, only in hundreds, and there they yet celebrated the ancient pagan ceremonies.

'One day,' Brendan often said, 'I shall go back to my islands.'

In the end it was to the lonely island of Inchiquin, in Loch Corrib, he went. There he wrote down the story of his travels and there he died, going on his last voyage to the Isles of the Blest.

# 6

## COLUMCILLE, DOVE OF
## THE CHURCH

## Columcille

He was like a prince and proud,
Like all his gallant race;
Yet he laid the warrior's sword
And chose the way of grace.

He was learned and wise,
An eagle in his looks
And, when he went travelling,
He carried only books.

Saint Finnian had a precious book
And scholars from all lands
Gathered at Clonard to admire
This work of holy hands.

And some told noble Columcille
Of this book so fine and rare.
'Sure, Finnian will let me read
And make a copy fair.

'For, while in Ireland there is one
Who cannot write or read,
I will not rest! More books! More books!
The saint and scholar need!'

He knelt before Saint Finnian
And begged that he might make
Two books where only one had been
For holy wisdom's sake.

'Come read and welcome: read again,'
The great Saint Finnian said.
'But two instead of one? No! No!'
He slowly shook his head.

Only the silent shadows watched
While Colum wrote throughout the night,
Letter by letter, ink and colour,
Complete at last, by morning's light.

But now a spy the story tells
Of how he saw the candle dim
Gleam through the night – and there's the proof!
Page upon page – prayer, psalm and hymn.

' 'Tis mine!' cried Finnian. Erin's king
Upheld him. Out through Tara's door,
Up to the north went Columcille
Calling Clan Neill to war.

Fight for the book! Sword against sword
On for O'Neill! the battle cry.
North against South and Columcille
Saw clan and king's men die.

Too late he grieved. 'For me they died.
My sin is great. This fearful wrong
I brought on Erin. I – a priest!
My penance must be hard and long.

'Put out the boat,' said Columcille.
'I am not worthy here to stay.
An exile I from my own land,
Until my sin is purged away.'

He went across the stormy sea
To where the misty islands rise;
Savage and black the mountains grey,
Drear to his sorrowful eyes.

Yet in his exile he was great.
The wilderness he tamed and taught.
He conquered heathens with the Cross
And set old wrongs at naught.

# KNIGHTS OF GOD

He came back once, for the poets' sake,
To save them from the wrath of kings
And people. For, without the word,
The deed is but a thing of wings

That flashes once across the light
Once only and is seen no more.
Destroy the poets and the past
Is gone for evermore.

Of all our noble exiles,
The glory of Ireland still –
Warriors, saints and poets –
None greater than Columcille.

# COLUMCILLE

♣

## *Columba at School*

ONE hundred years after Patrick carried the Cross to
Tara, a boy named Columba was living with his foster
father, the priest Cruithnechan, at the foot of the Donegal
mountains.

Today it is a wild, lonely place, where ravens build
their nests and stoats and badgers roam the woods. When
Columba lived there he could hear wolves howling at
night and often he saw a golden eagle, with great wings
outspread, flying towards the sun.

He loved wild animals, even the wolves, so he had no
fear of them. He made pets of squirrels, and on his walks
was followed by birds flying and fluttering round him.

His mother was of royal blood and his father was descended from Niall of the Nine Hostages, the warrior
king, who captured Saint Patrick and made him a
slave.

When Columba was old enough to begin learning to
read, Cruithnechan had a cake made every day marked
with the letters of the alphabet. The little boy sat on the
bank of the stream which flowed down the mountain in
front of his home, dabbled his feet in the water as he ate
his cake and sang the letters over and over again until he
knew them.

There were other boys in the charge of the priest and
they called Columba, Columcille, or 'Dove of the
Church', because he was so gentle and always seemed to
be coming from the church.

Those who noticed his gentleness, forgot that Columcille came of a long line of warriors and that he was re-

markably brave for a child. But they remembered it later.

After a few years Columcille went to live in Leinster with a bard, and from him he learned the old stories and poems of Ireland. Soon he was making poems himself and became a member of the Order of Bards. His poems were so good and so well liked that they were written out and copied again and again. Some of them have come down to our own time.

As soon as he was grown up, Columcille left his poet teacher and went to Saint Finnian's famous monastic school at Clonard, where he became a priest.

One of Columcille's kinsmen gave him a dun in the middle of an oak wood. Here he made a great clearing, and built his first church. There is a town there now and they called it Derry, which means the oak wood.

He loved building churches and copying manuscripts. He had a great love of learning and, as copying was the only way books could be increased, he copied all he could. He was a very quick writer and is said to have finished three hundred manuscripts.

Columcille welcomed the students who came in hundreds to Ireland from Europe, where the Huns, Goths and Vandals were trying to destroy civilization. His colleges were groups of wooden huts built around the church, each new student putting up his own hut. His royal kinsmen were very proud of him, for he was adding to the fame of Ireland and of the church. Yet some of them thought he was more fitted to be a soldier than a priest, for he was tall and straight, very strong, and with clear grey eyes.

'He is fearless, can handle men and comes of a royal race, and we could make him King!' they said.

# The Precious Book

A young student staying at Columcille's college, on his way to the West, declared that among Saint Finnian's collection of manuscripts was one of the finest he had ever seen.

'It's far better than anything you have here!' he told Columcille.

'Saint Finnian,' cried Columcille. 'You mean Saint Finnian of Clonard?'

'I do, indeed!' said the student. 'Isn't it a pity you haven't a copy of the book here?'

Columcille laughed.

'That's easily arranged. I will copy it myself! I was at school under Saint Finnian. He loves books almost as much as I do and he'll be only too pleased for another copy to be made.'

He set out at once for Clonard. There weren't trains, or buses or motor-cars in Ireland then, but Irish people were always travelling, in chariots, on horses, and, if they had neither chariot nor horse, they went on foot. There were sailing boats and currachs in every port and on every river.

Saint Finnian was proud of his old pupil and welcomed him to Clonard. They sat talking about old times, what had happened to the other boys who were at school with Columcille and the terrible state of the world outside Ireland.

Columcille told how he had heard of Saint Finnian's precious book.

'I'd be very glad to have a copy of it in my own library,' said Columcille.

The old man leaned back in his chair and shook his head.

'You can read it while you are here and I hope you will stay a very long time. You can study the manuscript, but you must not copy it,' said Saint Finnian.

'But – ' began Columcille. Then he stopped. He remembered that Saint Finnian never changed his mind. He was clever, generous, but obstinate.

Columcille was obstinate too.

'There should be more books!' he thought indignantly. 'There can't be too many and Saint Finnian knows as well as I do that the only way to increase the number of books is to copy them. All over Ireland people are learning to read and they need books.'

Late into the night he strode up and down the cell where he was lodged, trying to think of some way of persuading Finnian to let him copy the manuscript.

'I'll give him anything I have. I'll make two copies if he'll let me have one,' he muttered. 'But I must have that one!'

The next day Saint Finnian showed Columcille the new buildings, the fine stone wall, and then he showed him his library.

There were far more manuscripts in it than Columcille ever hoped to possess. Saint Finnian was so friendly that Columcille could not believe he would still refuse, so he asked him again.

'Copy anything else you wish and do not hurry over the work. Stay till you can stay no longer, but do not ask what has already been refused,' Saint Finnian told him.

Like all the O'Neills, Columcille was very proud. He was ashamed that he had asked twice. Leaving Saint Finnian without a word, he went back to his cell, determined to leave Clonard at once.

But he could not go without a copy of that precious book.

'Why should he refuse?' he asked himself. 'It isn't to be understood. 'Tis true that Finnian is old and he always was unreasonable, but he does love learning, and all I ask is that where there is one book I shall make two.'

He sat in his cell until all around him the monks and students were asleep. He stared out from the door towards the building where Finnian kept his manuscripts. The night was dark. There was no moon. Not a light shone in the whole place. Far off a dog barked and answering cries came from the forest.

Slowly Columcille walked across the enclosure. A leather satchel swung from a strap over his shoulder. In it he kept his parchments, pens and inks, his paints and a flint for striking a light; a good, thick candle too, made of mixed beef and mutton fat.

The great oak door of the library was latched but not chained. There were no thieves inside the monastery walls.

Yet, like a thief, Columcille noiselessly opened the door, entered and closed it behind him. He struck a light, fixed his candle on a stone slab and took down the manuscript he had determined to copy.

It was a wonderful piece of work. Each capital letter was in colour, with tiny drawings in the curves and loops. Columcille laid it on a desk and turned the pages.

'An artist who loved God made this book!' he said aloud.

He settled to his task.

All night he worked. His hand was stiff with grasping the pen; his head ached; his eyes were closing with weariness when he heard the crowing of a cock.

Starting up, he saw that darkness was fading A pale light was coming into the sky. Dawn was breaking. Soon everyone in Clonard would be up, washing, cleaning, cooking and all praying as they worked. The boys in the school would be yawning and stretching, pleading for another ten minutes, then rushing out into the chill morning air.

The candle wick, the tiny scrap that was still unburned, sank sideways in the melted grease and spluttered out. Columcille scraped it off the stone and, dropping it on the floor, ground what was left of the candle into the rushes strewn on the earth. He replaced the manuscript, gathered up his parchments, his brushes, pens and ink, and went swiftly out. As he reached his cell the great bell rang. Another moment and he would have been discovered.

'I must not work so long,' he decided. 'There are some who rise before dawn to pray. The risk is too great!'

The next night, the following night and the night after that, Columcille wrote and painted, drawing with such care and skill that he knew his copy would be far better than the original book.

During the day he taught in the school, made poems, studied, and slept all he could. Like the other monasteries of Ireland, Clonard had many guests and no one wondered that Columcille should stay so long.

The night came when Columcille copied the last page, the last line. Where there had been one book there were now two. He laid down his pen and leaned back, happy that he had worked so well.

His candle was burning clearly and the tiny light shone out into the night. A shepherd, returning from the fold, saw the gleam and, fearing that robbers were stealing Saint Finnian's precious books, crept close up and peeped in.

He could see a monk sitting at a desk with two books before him. He remembered that the famous Psalter was kept there and that the Abbot had forbidden anyone to copy it.

'Why should a man work secretly at night unless he is doing something forbidden?' thought the shepherd. 'Saint Finnian is my master. I will not have him wronged!'

He was about to cry out and raise the alarm. Changing his mind, he slipped away and beat on Finnian's door.

Finnian heard the story in silence, but he was furious.

'Bring Columcille before me!' he ordered.

Columcille came, marching like a soldier, his head thrown back, his grey eyes flashing.

'You asked if you might make a copy of the Psalter of Clonard,' said Finnian.

'I did!' agreed Columcille.

'And I refused!' declared Finnian. 'You have disobeyed me, but since the work is done I demand the copy.'

'The copy is mine!' cried Columcille. 'I have made the world richer. Other copies shall be made and the sacred learning will spread through Ireland.'

'I will appeal to the King!' said Finnian. 'He shall decide between us!'

All the priests, nobles and poets of Ireland who could reach Tara were assembled there when Diarmuid, the King, was to decide between Finnian and Columcille.

Saint Finnian spoke first. He was old and his voice trembled, yet anger made it clear and piercing.

'The book is mine!' he said. 'I had it written. 'Twas my money paid for the smoothest parchments, the clearest ink and the finest ground paints that should make it beautiful. The leather for the cover came from my tannery, the binding was done in my workshop. The book is one of the glories of Clonard! Students and scholars from the most distant parts of Europe have come to study in my library.

I made them welcome. I made Columcille welcome. He was my pupil. I was proud of him. When he asked permission to copy my Book of Psalms and I refused, I could not believe he would disobey me. Columcille has betrayed my hospitality! The book is mine. It was copied against my wish. Therefore the copy is mine too!'

'Finnian is right!' cried so many it seemed that everyone in that great hall agreed with him. Yet there were some who shook their heads.

'We will listen to Columcille,' they murmured.

Columcille stood up taller than the men around him, and so straight and fierce amid all these learned men that they remembered he might have been a soldier or even king.

'I have built churches!' cried Columcille. 'They are the monuments of our faith. But without the words and teaching of the Church what meaning would they have for us? It is the written books that matter, and we have so few. All over Ireland men and women are crying out for learning. We have saints and scholars, but we could have more! Where I have found a book, I have always copied it, so that always I was bringing more books into the world. Saint Finnian's book is precious. I did not rob him of it. I did not harm it. Only now there are two. I am willing that my book shall belong to Ireland! Any man or woman who can read shall have that copy laid open to study freely. But I will not give it up to Finnian! No! I will not give the toil of nights to Finnian who refused his consent. I will not!'

His keen eyes flashed round on that crowded hall and shouts and cries answered him –

'The copy is yours, Columcille! The copy is yours!'

The noise ceased. All looked at Diarmuid, who sat on his throne, troubled and anxious.

It was a long time before he spoke.

'Here is my judgement – the book was Finnian's. He had the right to refuse or to consent. He refused. Therefore the copy is his. I follow the law – to every cow its calf. That is my judgement, Columcille, and you must abide by it. Give the copy to Finnian!'

Finnian sat back in his chair and smiled. He was glad he had won and yet he felt sorry. Perhaps he wished he had given permission.

Columcille carried the book under his arm. He opened it and turned the pages he had copied night after night. Then he laid it at the King's feet.

'This is an unjust decision, Diarmuid. It is a slur on my honour. I who am a scholar, a holy priest, and a man of royal blood! Finnian will have the copy I made, but Ireland will hear more of this book. I call on the O'Neills!'

'You threaten me?' demanded Diarmuid.

Columcille did not answer. He stared back at the King with angry eyes, then turned away.

He strode as far as the door. But there armed men seized him and he was hurried away until the frightened King could make up his mind what to do with him.

'You must advise me!' Diarmuid told Finnian.

They talked and planned, and while they talked, Columcille had forced the door of his prison, climbed the wall of the dun and was travelling north, night and day, towards Tyrconnell. He did not go direct but stopped at every town and village, or collection of huts on the way. From each he sent a messenger to his clan, the O'Neills.

He knew he would be followed and he watched at every bend of the road. When he stayed for food or rest, he went only with those he could trust. He did not take the high road, but the paths that only herdsmen and the cutters of wood and turf knew.

He was crossing the mountains and was feeling very lonely and desolate when a hymn came into his mind:

> Alone I am on the mountain,
> O King's son of the lucky road,
> There is nothing for me to dread.
> It is not with chance our life is
> Or with the bird on top of the twig.
> It is better to put our trust in
> The Father, the One and the Son.

## Battle for the Book

As Columcille came down from the mountains a line of war chariots crowded with young men carrying spears and swords came swinging along to meet him.

'Hail, O'Neill!' they cried.

'I am Colum of the Church!' answered Columcille. 'If you have come to help me, remember – I blame Diarmuid, not Finnian.'

'There is an army coming up!' they told him. 'Each soldier in that army is an O'Neill. Every O'Neill in Ulster and in Connaught will march to Tara. Even the High King shall not do an injustice to an O'Neill!'

'The King will not fight!' said Columcille. 'When he realizes that we are determined he will give me back my book.'

But Diarmuid did fight. With the royal army he met the O'Neills at Cuil Dremhue, near Sligo. He attacked, but three thousand of his men fell beneath the spears and swords of the O'Neills.

Columcille believed that the King would yield before the armies met. He was returning to make a last appeal to Finnian when he heard that fighting had commenced.

He turned his chariot round at once and, stopping only

to change horses, drove on until he reached Cuil Dremhue.

He arrived too late to stop the battle, and when he saw the dead and dying on the field, he was horror-stricken.

'What have I done?' he cried. 'It is I who have killed my own countrymen. I am unworthy to be an Irishman!

'This is where my pride has led me! Why did I not submit to Finnian? Why did I not submit to the King? I thought I was a follower of Christ. I do not deserve to live in Ireland!'

The High King's troops were retreating, but Columcille stopped the march of the O'Neills. Diarmuid fled to Tara and shut himself up there. He was not pursued.

'Go back!' said Columcille to the O'Neills. 'You have proved your friendship. But I have been wrong. Tomorrow I leave Ireland for ever!'

## The Exile

In little, hide-covered boats, Columcille and the few friends he allowed to go with him set sail for the Hebrides. They were almost swamped in a terrible whirlpool, the Cauldron of Brechan, but the light, strong boats carried them to safety where far stronger and heavier vessels had been dragged down.

They passed the rocky islands of Islay and Jura, and put in at Oronsay. The voyage had been rough and they were all thankful to be on land again.

'A man might do worse than live here!' said one of the monks, as they lit a fire and put on a saucepan to warm some food. 'There's good stone here to build cells and an oratory. That sea looks fine for fishing, though I've heard the mists are terrible.'

Columcille was restless. He left the camp and climbed a hill. He looked at the rocky islands they had passed and beyond them to the whirlpool where they had nearly been destroyed. He raised his eyes and there, across the sea, were the blue mountains of Ireland rising out of the stormy waves.

Down he went from the hill.

'We cannot stay!' he cried. 'Ireland is still in sight. I would spend my days and nights looking towards those shores. We must go farther!'

They did not stay to rest, but made a hasty meal and stepped once more into their boats.

They came to Iona, and then indeed Ireland could not be seen even by Columcille's strong eyes. When he looked out and saw nothing but the rocky islands and the narrow, treacherous seas of that coast, he knew he was at last in exile. A heap of stones still marks the place and is called the Cairn of Farewell.

The little bay where their boats anchored is named Port a Churaich or the Bay of the Coracle.

As they stepped from their boats, the exiles felt they would love Iona. The air was sweet with thyme and the fields rich with clover. There were gentle slopes for the growing of corn, a harbour for their boats, and on the mainland, the pagan Picts for them to convert to Christianity.

'We did well to come here!' said Columcille.

The monks set to work at once to build huts of wood and wattle facing the large island of Mull, a guest-house, a refectory and a church.

They drew up a list of rules. Columcille, like Patrick and Brigid, insisted on hospitality, and kindness to animals.

The Picts were the last people to believe in the Druid

religion. Brude, King of the Picts, had his fortress right on the other side of Alba, which we call Scotland, where Inverness now stands.

The monks made friends with savage fishermen who had ventured out to spy on the islanders. It was from these Columcille learned about Brude and determined to go to him.

The Pictish fortress was a hundred and fifty miles away through mountainous country but, the moment the settlement was built, Columcille prepared a boat. He chose six monks to go with him and, loading some food on board, Columcille set out.

The mountains were grey and bleak, with thick, cold mists sweeping over them. From the moment they left Iona until they reached the end of their expedition, the seven adventurers were soaked with cold rain and mist. They never found a dry spot to camp in, and they believed they had discovered a land where the sun never shone.

As they rowed their boats up the narrow lochs Columcille sang his Hymn of Protection. The monks forgot they were in a strange country where wild beasts, and savages as wild and fierce, inhabited the desolate gorges which pierced the mountains.

Between the lochs were strips of marshy land where they waded knee-deep among the rushes, dragging the boat behind them. There were no paths but rocky barriers where they stumbled along, carrying it on their shoulders. They were fortunate that it was one of the lightest of the hide-covered currachs, or they would never have reached the end of their journey.

At night they were happy if they could find enough dry wood to make a fire. They crouched in caves where the floors streamed with water and the roofs dripped. Their bread went mouldy; their bones ached and they shivered in the damp cold.

They never thought of turning back. They laughed and planned, and Columcille reminded them that the greater their struggles and privations the more glorious would be their victory.

Their food was finished. They hadn't the strength to search for more. They were covered with scratches and bruises. Their clothes hung on them in rags. They left the currach at the last loch and, stumbling with weariness and hunger, came to the fortress of King Brude.

He had been warned of their coming. From behind rocks and from the tops of mountains the Picts had watched every step of this amazing expedition. They had shot at Columcille and his followers with heavy, flint-tipped arrows, had rolled down rocks to stop their passage and crush the boat.

The monks, chanting hymns to keep up their courage, scarcely pausing for rest lest their provisions should give out, weak and unarmed, had succeeded. Before them lay the stronghold of the Picts!

The gates were closed. Columcille marched straight up to them.

'Open – King Brude! Open to the messenger of Christ!' he cried.

They were watched from the walls, yet no voice answered and the gates remained shut.

Columcille traced a cross on the enormous bars of wood with his finger. The bolts shot back, the gate swung open, and the little company of monks entered the fortress.

Once inside, King Brude welcomed them. He admired this tall, determined stranger who had led his followers through such dangerous ways.

'Such a man's religion must be fine and worth knowing!' he decided.

The Druids were hostile. But soon Columcille was preaching all round Inverness. The story of his wonderful march to the gates of King Brude was told at every camp fire, in every dwelling, and the people came to hear him. The Druids frightened them. Columcille made them brave and happy.

Fishermen, who had built their huts among the rocks on the islands of the Hebrides, heard of the great Irish saint and wondered would they ever see him. They went down to their nets and there, coming over the waves, was the leather-covered boat, dancing in its eagerness, with the man who had converted their king standing up in it. He sailed away to the Orkneys and Shetlands, north to the Faroes and even to Iceland, where he saw the sun at midnight and volcanoes throwing up stones and fire.

While he travelled, Columcille made songs about ships on the sea, sea-gulls and cormorants, songs for fishermen and, along the shores of Scotland, men going out in the night to cast their nets, still sing the songs Columcille made for them. He was called the Troubadour of Ireland.

These Irish exiles brought their love of learning with them to Iona and, when Columcille came back from his wanderings, he would find boats anchored in the harbour and people from distant lands going on shore to study with the monks, or setting sail again when they had learnt all they could.

For a while Columcille stayed in Iona. He was studying navigation, for he believed in skill as well as in prayer. It was pleasant to walk about the island, followed by his pet

crane, and helping in the everyday work of the settlement. He was beginning to wonder where he should go next when a message came to him. It was from the poets of Ireland.

'Come home and protect us. We are attacked!' was the message. 'You are a poet too!'

The poets in Ireland had great power. They told the stories of the kings and queens, and the great ones of the land. They sat at the high table. They had wealth and honour. Some grew so proud and unreasonable that the people rose against them and demanded of the king that they should be banished.

'I vowed never to see my own country again!' said Columcille. 'I caused one battle by my pride and anger. If I could make peace it would be well to go.'

So Columcille went back to Ireland. But he would not break his word. When the Mountains of Mourne were like clouds on the horizon he blindfolded himself with a handkerchief so that he could not see them. He heard the waves breaking on the shore: he felt the springy turf under his feet and the air was scented with gorse and heather as he remembered it. The poets were there to meet him and began at once to complain of their harsh treatment.

'Don't you deserve it?' asked Columcille. 'Is there a poet in Ireland who did not think it should be two cows if he had been given one? Four pieces of gold instead of two? I have heard that the King feared he would be left without house or land if the poets had their way. I have heard, too, that the people, who used to bless and praise us for the joy our poems gave them, now hate and condemn the poets of Ireland. Is this true?'

The poets were silent.

'So it is true!' said Columcille. 'I dare not blame you, for I did more wrong to Ireland than you will ever do.'

'And you will speak for us at the Convention at Drumceat?' demanded the poets.

'I will speak for you!' agreed Columcille.

When he was led into the banqueting hall, the nobles

gathered there stared in amazement at the bandage over his eyes.

Knowing the poets had appealed to him, they had wondered if he would come. Columcille had never broken his word – never! And he had vowed never to see Ireland again. Now they understood. There wasn't one of them, from the King down to the young girl standing behind the Queen, that didn't feel desperately sorry.

'You have been asked to banish the poets from Ireland,' said Columcille, speaking to the King. 'They are blamed for their pride and greed, and no doubt among them, there are those who love the rewards of poetry more than poetry itself.'

'That's true!' cried his listeners, all speaking at once. 'They'd take the two eyes out of your head! They'd not leave the thatch on a poor man's cabin, or a drink at a wedding feast! Thieves and robbers – that's the poets of Ireland!'

'Silence!' roared the King. 'Silence for Columcille!'

'Every word you say may be true,' went on Columcille. 'But you, King and Queen, you nobles and ladies, have you thought what will happen if you banish the poets? When great deeds are done – who will tell of them? When a lady is beautiful, or has great wisdom, only her friends and neighbours will know. When a King dies, who will record his reign? You will, all of you, be forgotten in a few years. The poets are our memory: the poets keep alive the story of our race!'

The poets were delighted.

But Columcille had something to say to them as well.

'As for you, poets and bards of Ireland, you should have the pride that gives, not takes. In the homes of the poor you should leave presents as well as songs behind you. In the halls of the rich take care that any gift shall seem small compared with the value of your work!'

He went out from the hall and he was never seen again in Ireland.

Columcille was growing old and the most welcome of all his guests were those who came from Ireland. Like Saint Patrick and Saint Brigid he loved birds and animals. He told a monk one day that in three days' time a stork from Ireland would come to visit him.

'Watch for him and take care of him,' he said. 'My guest will be exhausted when he comes.'

The monk was as fond of birds as was Columcille. He kept a look-out and, on the third day, a stork, driven and beaten by the winds, dropped upon the rocky shore. The monk lifted it carefully and carried it to the guest-house. There he smoothed its feathers, gave it food and drink and a soft bed. For three days it rested, then flew back to Ireland on a calm day, while Columcille watched its flight until he could see it no longer.

A great friend of Columcille's was an old white horse who carried the milk pails from the dairy to the monastery. Often Columcille walked with it and used to talk as though to a brother monk. Every day Columcille walked a little slower. He began to sit down and rest half-way. After a few times the horse put its head on Columcille's shoulder and big tears streamed from its eyes. The monks, busy about the dairy, looked on in amazement.

'You are wise and holy men,' said Columcille, 'but my friend the horse knows more than you. He is saying good-bye to me.'

A few days after, Columcille died on the altar of his own chapel, smiling with joy.

# 7

## KEVIN
## OF GLENDALOUGH

## Kevin

The lakes of Glendalough are dark;
The rocks around are steep
As when Saint Kevin weary lay
On the sodden earth to sleep.

He had no home, no friend nor guide;
He journeyed quite alone,
Yet gentle eyes were watching him
From every bush and stone.

The birds and beasts of Glendalough
Drew nearer one by one.
When Kevin wakened from his dreams
They did not fly nor run.

Where Kevin walked they followed him,
And, when he knelt in prayer,
Only the wind and waterfalls
Disturbed the quiet air.

For Kevin loved all birds, the hare,
The red fox in his den
And hunted boar, or frightened deer,
Found refuge in the glen.

# KEVIN OF GLENDALOUGH

♣

### Kevin of the Angels

KEVIN'S earliest home was at the Fort of the White Fountain in Wicklow. In Irish, Kevin is Coemghen, the beautiful or fair-begotten, and he was a very lovely child. Indeed, all his family were famous for their good looks.

When Kevin was being baptized, the priest, looking up, saw twelve angels standing by the font, each angel carrying a lighted candle. So they called the child Kevin of the Angels.

Kevin was seven years old when he was given into the care of Saint Petroc, who came from Cornwall. Afterwards Petroc went back to his own place and founded a monastic school which was called Petroc-stowe, now known as Padstow. Kevin was with him for twelve years. Then he studied with his uncle Eugenius at Kilnamanagh. After a while Eugenius wanted to go up to his mother's territory in the north to preach there.

'The trouble is,' he said, 'to find someone to take my place. I choose Kevin, though he is so young. I heard that where he lived as a child, the air was bitter and a cold wind always blew. Yet while he was there the people knew only Spring. Kevin must be more than usually good.'

Kevin heard this and dreaded the responsibility.

'I am not fit to be head of a monastery,' he thought. 'Haven't they older men, wiser and more learned?'

That night Kevin fled from the monastery into the Wicklow mountains. Rain fell in gusts as he went softly out of the gate, and soon he was wet through. There was no moon, and the only paths were those made by the goats and mountain sheep. His sandals were loose and he slipped on the stones. Once he saw stars reflected in water far below and clung to a rock.

He was so weary he sat in the shelter of a twisted thorn-bush growing from the rock. He was bruised, his robe was tattered, his head nodded, but he dared not sleep. He found a track which led downwards and stumbled along.

The track wound upwards, then down again. The way would have been far shorter had he taken the road by the Avonmore River, but Kevin felt safer in the mountains.

When morning came, a dreary, windswept morning, Kevin reached a dark, narrow valley. All around rose the steep mountains. At one end it opened on the river. Streams poured down the rocks and fell into two long lakes. The air was filled with dancing spray, and the music of waterfalls was louder than the song of the many birds which perched in the trees.

If Kevin looked up he saw fluttering wings. If he looked down, the sunlight flashing on the black surface of the lakes bewildered him.

'This must be Glendalough,' said Kevin. 'God brought me here, and here I will stay.'

Though the valley was beautiful, it seemed a chill, desolate spot. Kevin found a great hollow tree which had been uprooted in a storm. Dead leaves had drifted in, and there he sheltered from wind and rain. Great clusters of blackberries, juicy and sweet as grapes, swung from the brambles, and the biggest hazel nuts he had ever seen loaded the bushes.

'A house, food, and all the water in the lakes! What more do I need?' asked Kevin.

In his wanderings through the valley Kevin came upon a cave on the north side where the cliff overhangs the water. It was so low Kevin could not stand upright in it and so narrow there was little room to move. But he stretched himself there and gazed into the lake thirty feet below.

He built a hut of green branches and, when he sat there, birds swarmed on the trees and watched him with their bright, curious eyes. When they grew used to him, the friendliest fluttered to his shoulders and sang without fear.

He was happy in his solitude, though he knew it would not last.

At the end of a long day, a huntsman with his hounds followed a wild boar through the mountains. They had come a great distance, for the boar did not stand and front his enemies, but fled towards Glendalough.

The rider and his horse were weary. Some of the hounds limped and whimpered uneasily. But the boar was lagging. He turned once and glared at his pursuers, then forced himself on.

'The mountains will be too much for him! I have never failed yet,' boasted the huntsman.

But he did not like the darkness, for the towering rocks and the dense bushes shut out the light which still showed in the sky. He longed for a warm, comfortable seat at a fire, with food and pleasant talk. He began to look over his shoulder and started at shadows.

Suddenly he discovered that the boar had disappeared. The hounds hung back and refused to follow. The man jumped from his horse, then drew back, for he stood on the edge of a cliff and right beneath him glimmered the dark waters of a lake he had never seen before.

'But where's the boar?' he wondered.

He could hear no other sound but the splashing of waterfalls and the singing of birds.

'I never heard birds sing that way before!' muttered the huntsman. 'It's like listening to a choir.'

The singing came from one spot. Tethering his horse to a tree, he trod softly, and parting the branches carefully, so that not a twig cracked, he worked his way through the trees, the hounds keeping close and silent.

He came out upon a smooth circle of grass. At the edge a hut of branches was backed by nut bushes. Sitting on a log before it was a young man in the robe of a monk. Birds flew in and out of the hut, they crowded the trees and perched on the young monk's shoulders. A blackbird was pecking seed from his outstretched hand.

On the grass beside the hut the boar lay peaceful and untroubled. The hounds stretched out, making no attempt to attack their former enemy.

'Is this an angel I see?' asked the huntsman in wonder, for the monk's face was grave and handsome, while his eyes, when he looked up, were filled with great happiness.

The huntsman ventured forward.

'Welcome!' said Kevin. 'Welcome as the poor boar you chased. Here is sanctuary for man and beast!'

'Are you an angel?' and the rough huntsman took off his cap.

'I am Kevin, the hermit,' the other told him. 'Rest. Then I will show you a short way home.'

'I will never hunt in these mountains,' promised the huntsman. 'But I will come again.'

'Please God you will,' said Kevin.

A farmer whose land lay on the far side of the mountains had one miserable cow, all skin and bone. The land was poor, and the scanty grass gave the poor creature so little nourishment she strayed into the mountains. There she came upon Kevin with birds hovering in the air around him and the wild animals of the woods following as he drew water and gathered sticks.

The cow pushed aside the deer, the badgers and foxes and pressed against Kevin. He stroked her smooth head.

The cow licked his hand, then began to graze on the short, thick grass by the hut, and went back home when the valley grew dark.

Every day the cow came to Kevin's hut. Every day she licked his hand in greeting, and he began to look out for her.

'I'll have a cow of my own one of these days,' he decided.

The farmer saw that his cow was getting fatter. Her milk was rich, and soon he was boasting of the cream and butter he had.

'There must be grand pasture in the mountains,' he told his wife, and he followed the cow to discover where she went.

He came upon Kevin as he prayed, with the wild birds and the animals keeping quiet among the trees.

'You must be a saint!' cried the farmer, falling on his knees. 'Give me your blessing!'

The huntsman told of what he had seen and the farmer talked about his cow. In time the King of Leinster heard of Kevin and his love for animals. The King's favourite falcon had broken its wing and no one dared to go near it. The fierce bird screamed with pain and refused to eat.

At last its master sent to Kevin and implored him to help the injured bird. Kevin took the falcon in his hands, bound up the wing and coaxed it to eat from his fingers. Soon it was able to fly back to the King.

When Kevin came to Glendalough there were a few rough tracks leading into the valley. Now so many came to ask his blessing, to tell him their troubles and listen to his advice, that their feet trampled a wide road.

Many monks came and begged him to let them stay. They built a beautiful oratory on a rock thrusting out upon the lake, and lived in huts scattered among the rocks.

Every day more monks arrived, and Kevin began to build a monastery farther down the valley.

While the stones were being shaped, an angel appeared to Kevin.

'Shall I smooth out the mountains and level the woods?' he asked. 'Your companions will need better food than the nuts and berries you like so well. I can make this valley the richest pasture land in Ireland.'

Kevin shook his head.

'And what would become of all the wild creatures on the mountains? They are my friends – loving and kind. They would be sad to hear you offer to destroy their homes.'

Kevin's monastery is lonely now. His oratory is a heap of stones. But his bare cell remains and, on the Wicklow mountains and in the trees, the wild creatures and the birds still live.

# 8

## LAWRENCE O'TOOLE
## CAPTIVE PRINCE

## Lawrence O'Toole

He was hostage to Dermot MacMurrough,
MacMurrough na Gall*.
A brave, fearless boy he was taken
Out from his father's hall.

Into the tyrant's keeping
The little hostage went.
So early he knew sorrow
And all that sorrow meant.

Rescued from MacMurrough
To Glendalough he came.
And, as the years passed slowly
All Ireland learned his name.

Now a great man in Dublin,
Archbishop Lawrence saw
The people he loved turned outcast
With neither land nor law.

King Rory in his castle,
The nobles in their forts
Had little care for Ireland,
Nor honour in their thoughts.

But Lawrence rode throughout the land –
'Unite! Unite!' he cried.
'For Church and Country arm and fight!'
He would not be denied.

A hostage in his boyhood:
A patriot to the end:
A saint who struggled all his days
His country to defend.

*MacMurrough of the Strangers

# LAWRENCE O'TOOLE

♣

## *He sees MacMurrough*

LAWRENCE O'TOOLE was climbing the boundary wall when he heard the sound of horses' hooves on the road beyond. He scrambled the last bit in a hurry, too excited to think of his bruised knees and scraped shoes.

He pulled himself to the top. Then, leaning his elbows on the stones, felt about with his feet for a resting place and peeped over.

He nearly dropped back, for the road was crowded with armed men and, riding at their head on a huge black horse, was a man in armour.

The man's hand rested on his sword-hilt and he had pushed back the light steel cap he wore. The boy could see his dark, fierce face, with the curled plume nodding above it. When he turned in the saddle it seemed impossible that those blazing eyes should not notice the young watcher on the wall.

Archers and swordsmen, men carrying battle-axes on their shoulders, they marched steadily down the road. Lawrence waited there till they were out of sight. Letting himself down, he started running towards his father's castle.

Castle Dermot, The O'Toole's home, was hidden by trees. Long before he could reach it the boy heard shouts, the clash of steel meeting steel and the twanging of bows.

'The men I saw can't have reached the castle yet!' he thought in amazement. Indeed, when he paused to listen, he could still hear the tramp of men on the road.

Slipping from tree to tree he was in time to see the great

door of the castle flung open and the besiegers, headed by the dark horseman, enter.

The O'Tooles had been taken by surprise. The hospitable gates of their courtyard stood open day and night. A small advance guard had rushed these and only a few of The O'Toole's men had been ready to defend themselves.

By the time the dark horseman rode up, the prince was a prisoner in the hands of his enemies. They raced from room to room, killing those who offered resistance and taking possession of the castle.

Peering out from the trees Lawrence could tell that something terrible was happening. He did not know what to do. He might have taken shelter in one of the cabins beyond the walls, for the O'Tooles were well-liked, but he wanted to be with his father.

Lawrence was only ten years old, yet he had courage. Making up his mind, he came out of the shelter of the trees and had taken one step towards the castle when a hand gripped his arm, and a soldier who had crept up behind him laughed at the boy's startled face.

'Here's the young eagle!' he cried joyfully. 'You're wanted yonder, lad!'

Thrusting Lawrence before him, he tramped down to the gates, across the courtyard and in at the battered door.

The hall was crowded. The dark man was seated in the prince's chair, while The O'Toole and his three elder sons, their hands bound, stood before him.

When Lawrence appeared, they looked at him with pity and he tried to run to his father. His captor held the boy firmly and, though he kicked and struggled, the man easily managed him with one hand.

'So, here's the hostage!' said the dark man, leaning

forward in his chair. 'Well, O'Toole, if you value this lad's life, beware how you act. One deed of rebellion; one day's delay in the tribute and he dies!'

'I'm in your power!' retorted The O'Toole. 'But Lorcan is only a child. Ill-treat him and you shall discover there is still power in Ireland to punish you, Dermot Mac-Murrough!'

Lawrence had heard of MacMurrough. Mac-Murrough the Ruthless, they called him, and he knew what being a hostage meant. He opened his mouth to cry out to his father not to let him be taken away, to save him from MacMurrough. Then he saw the anger and resentment in his father's eyes, his bound hands, and kept silent. He straightened his small shoulders, held up his head and looked back at MacMurrough without fear.

He had his reward when his father's hands were unbound and they said good-bye.

'My brave son!' declared O'Toole. 'You shall not be forgotten!'

MacMurrough put the boy before him on his black horse and Lawrence rode away with his father's enemy.

They rode without stopping, leaving the foot soldiers far behind, until they came to a stony, desolate waste. Beyond, on a hillside, rose a fortified building. The gates were open. Unlike The O'Toole's castle, armed men stood in groups, waiting MacMurrough's return.

As they had ridden along he had boasted to Lawrence that only a fool would allow himself to be taken by surprise.

MacMurrough stopped his horse.

'Jump down!' he told Lawrence.

The boy was stiff and stumbled as he reached the ground. A tall, ragged fellow pulled him to his feet.

'Keep him alive. I ask no more!' said MacMurrough, and galloped off laughing.

Lawrence gazed after him, then looked around in dismay. The barren waste stretched to the foot of the mountains, and on the edge of a stream was a hut built of unmortared stones. Not another dwelling, no trees, no animals were to be seen.

### The Stone Breaker

As MacMurrough entered his castle, the gates closed behind him and Lawrence turned to his companion, who watched him with an unfriendly grin.

'So you're an O'Toole,' he sneered. 'We don't think much of them in these parts. You'll make yourself useful while you're here – if you don't want to know the feel of a strap!'

He led the way to the hut. By the opening, which served both as door and window, was a rough cart, half-filled with stones. Inside, a fire burned in the middle of the floor and the smoke found its way out through a hole in the roof. A heap of rags in the corner, a tree trunk against the wall for seat and table, and some tools, lying on the floor, were all the furniture.

The man carried a sack on his back. He flung it down.

'Get supper, young prince!' he said. 'And mind you cook it well, for Conn the Stone Breaker was always a dainty feeder!'

Lawrence stared at him in bewilderment. Sometimes, when he had been fishing with his brothers, they had cooked the catch. But his part had been to collect dry branches for the fire. He had never even cleaned a fish.

Conn realized that the boy knew nothing of cooking. Grumbling, he emptied the sack and strewed its contents on the floor – a thick cake of bread, a piece of meat and some cheese.

He pulled out a round, black saucepan from a heap of wood beside the fire.

'Half fill that with water,' he growled. 'The sooner you learn to cook, the better for you.'

Lawrence went out to the stream. He stood there with the saucepan in his hand, wondering in which direction his home lay and if he dared try to steal off.

'Stir yourself!' shouted Conn from the hut, and Lawrence, glancing back, saw the stone breaker glaring after him.

Hurriedly he half filled the saucepan and ran back with it.

'When I tell ye to do something, do it at once!' shouted Conn, and he struck the boy with his clenched fist.

The stone breaker cut up the meat and, putting it in the saucepan, set it on the fire. While it simmered he broke a crust off the bread and flung it to Lawrence. He took down a jar of beer from a dark shelf, stretched himself on the tree trunk, and took great bites of bread and cheese, with long draughts of beer.

When the meat was cooked he ate it out of the saucepan with his fingers. He left a little of the broth and that, with the crust, was all Lawrence had to eat.

By this time it was dark in the hut. Conn stretched himself on the rags and groaned with weariness.

'I like me sleep,' he said. 'But I wake at the least noise. So don't think to escape, young O'Toole. Nothing has ever escaped me.'

He rolled over, and Lawrence sat on the floor by the fire, his head on his knees.

'I'll wait till he's asleep,' thought the boy. 'Then I'll run away.'

He waited. His eyes closed. He slipped to the floor and lay there as sound asleep as the man in the corner.

The next day the stone breaker made him load the cart with stones and help push it down to the road.

MacMurrough cared nothing for the kind of houses his people had, but the road leading to his castle had to be kept smooth and firm. The boy helped Conn fill holes with stones and tramp them down. By nightfall he was so tired he cared for nothing but sleep.

Soon his clothes were worn out, but no one bothered to give him new ones. His shoes dropped from his feet and he went barefoot. His hair was uncut and hung in a mat round his thin face. He was nearly always hungry, lonely and unhappy.

Sometimes he dreamed he was back in Castle Dermot. When he woke in the wretched hut and knew there stretched before him another day of hardship and unkindness, he wept silently, so that Conn should not hear him. He never saw MacMurrough, although he heard him riding by in the distance. And he never heard from home.

He had been taught to read and write, but he had not seen a manuscript since he had become a hostage. He had been learning to play the harp. Now he forgot the tunes and the words of the songs he used to sing with his brothers. He wondered how Conn could endure his life. But the stone breaker seemed quite content if he had plenty to eat and drink.

One day Conn left Lawrence gathering stones into a heap while he went off with the cart for provisions. He was quite sure now that the boy would make no attempt to escape.

A man in a grey cloak, riding a black mule, came along the path and stopped to watch the boy.

'Come here, child!' he called.

Lawrence obeyed. Conn had taught him to do as he was told at once.

'You're far too young for such heavy work!' exclaimed the man. 'Have you no parents to care for you?'

Lawrence looked up at him in wonder. It was so long since anyone had spoken kindly to him, he could scarcely understand the words.

'I have a father,' he said sorrowfully. 'But I think he has forgotten me.'

'What is your name, avic?' asked the stranger.

'Lawrence O'Toole,' replied the boy.

'Lawrence O'Toole! Lawrence O'Toole!' repeated the man. 'Surely not son of The O'Toole?'

'He is my father. I am hostage to MacMurrough,' the boy told him.

Far away Lawrence could hear the creaking and grinding which warned him that Conn was returning with a loaded cart.

'That's the stone breaker coming back,' he whispered. 'He'll beat me if he sees you talking to me.'

'Poor child!' said the man pityingly. 'I'll let The O'Toole know how his son is ill-treated. He's been working to get you home again, but who'd think Mac-Murrough could be so vindictive. Don't let out a word! I'm thinking you'll not be much longer with your stone breaker. God keep you!'

He rode away without once looking back, and Lawrence was still gazing after him when Conn came up.

'What's that ye're staring at?' demanded the stone breaker.

'A man on a black mule,' answered Lawrence.

'Did he speak to ye?'

Lawrence did not reply. The man had told him not to let out a word and he wouldn't. Conn didn't bother. He was used to the boy's silence.

'Get behind the cart and push!' he ordered. 'I'm wanting me supper.'

He gave Lawrence some meat and a piece of cheese as well as bread for his supper. But the boy was too happy to care what he ate. The stranger would tell his father and, one day when he was dragging the heavy cart down to the road, The O'Toole would come galloping along. He would be lifted up and carried away from his misery to that wonderful castle he had almost forgotten.

### Bishop of Glendalough

The next day and the day after that, Lawrence kept watch for the gorgeously dressed horseman who was to deliver him. The days passed, he saw no one but the stone breaker, and slowly he began to think the man who had promised to help him belonged to a dream.

'I'll be here always,' he thought.

It was months now since the stranger had talked to him. The cart seemed heavier than ever, and one misty morning when Conn tipped out the stones and went off for provisions, Lawrence determined to run away.

The moment Conn was out of sight the boy began to run in the opposite direction. He was sure he must be right because he was leaving the moor with its stones and the desolate hut behind. He kept on until he came to where four roads met.

He could no longer see the mountains. He could no longer see MacMurrough's castle. The mist hid everything, and Lawrence thought it a friendly mist because it shut away all he hated.

'Which way lies Castle Dermot?' he wondered, trying to remember which road they had taken when Mac-Murrough brought him here.

'Straight on!' he decided, though he wasn't really sure at all.

He ran until he heard the creaking and grinding of a cart coming towards him.

'Maybe I could ask?' he thought anxiously.

Suddenly the mist parted and there was Conn trudging towards him and grumbling as he pulled the cart.

Lawrence expected to be beaten, but Conn was only surprised.

'Who told ye MacMurrough had sent for ye?' he demanded. 'And how could ye tell this was the shortest way? Get along now! He's not the one to be kept waiting!'

Lawrence was too frightened to move.

'Get on me back!' said Conn.

The boy was so light the stone breaker ran all the way with him. A horse was waiting in the courtyard, saddled and bridled.

On the steps stood MacMurrough, as bitter and scowling as when Lawrence had last seen him.

'So we're losing you, young Lorcan!' he said. 'Yet I think you'll remember the time you were a hostage at Ferns.'

Lawrence looked at him without answering and MacMurrough, flushed with anger, strode into the castle.

As the sound of his footsteps ceased, Conn seized Lawrence and seated him on the horse.

'Ready!' he shouted.

A young man, quietly dressed and with a friendly look, jumped up behind the boy.

'Lean back,' he said. 'You'll ride the easier.'

Lawrence could scarcely speak.

'Are you taking me to my father?' he asked so softly the young man had to bend to hear him.

'To the Bishop of Glendalough,' he replied.

Lawrence sighed. He was terribly disappointed. Two big tears rolled down his cheeks and he let them fall.

The horse bounded across the courtyard, out through the gates between the staring soldiers and up the road across the mountains.

The young man was smiling.

'Your father heard how badly you were being treated. He has been threatening MacMurrough and at last he appealed to the Bishop. It has taken time. MacMurrough is too proud to return you to your father, but he has been forced to give you up to the Bishop. Your father is on his way to Glendalough and you'll see him there.'

Lawrence sighed again. This time with happiness.

They rode through the mountains, and the boy slept in his companion's arms. He woke when the horse's hooves clattered over a stone causeway and he saw before him the lighted windows of a monastery.

All the doors and gates were wide open and the music of bells floated down the gloomy valley.

A tall, old man, wearing long robes, came to meet them and held out his arms to Lawrence.

'Welcome, Lorcan O'Toole!' he said. 'Here you will never know unkindness or loneliness. And tomorrow you shall see your father!'

He led the boy into the warm, bright building. He was given a hot bath and new clothes. His hair was cut, and when he sat at supper in the clean refectory with the silent, friendly monks, Lawrence thought he must be in heaven.

That night he could not sleep. Lying on the dirty floor of the stone breaker's hut he had slept soundly. Now, in a clean bed, with friends all about him, he lay awake.

In the morning he walked through the gloomy valley with the Bishop. Lawrence did not think it gloomy. He listened as the Bishop talked of the trouble MacMurrough was bringing on the land with his fighting and raiding.

'Once,' he said, 'Ireland was called the Land of Saints and Scholars. There were monasteries and colleges in every district. Men and women loved learning and holiness. Ireland was wonderful in those days.'

As they went back Lawrence was thinking hard. He looked up at the Bishop's kind, serious face and wished he could stay with him always. Yet The O'Toole would soon be here to take him home. The boy loved his father but he felt he would never forget this walk.

The Bishop showed Lawrence where Saint Kevin had lived centuries ago.

'All about here,' he said, 'the people talk of Saint Kevin as if he were still alive!'

The dark lakes, the steep rocks with streams tumbling over them so that the air was filled with their splashing, looked serene in the morning sunlight, and now the bells were ringing all along the valley.

They were entering the monastery when the Bishop stopped and laid his hand on Lawrence's shoulder.

'Your father is coming!'

Four horsemen were galloping over the causeway. The man in front was The O'Toole. The three behind were only boys, and though Lawrence could scarcely remember them, he knew they were his brothers.

They sprang from their horses almost before they pulled up. The boys hung back while The O'Toole greeted his youngest son.

'My poor lad! How thin you are! Thank God you are out of MacMurrough's hands! My Lord Bishop! How can I show my gratitude? As I rode along I made up my mind that one of my sons shall become a priest. Shall we cast lots to decide which, for all three are willing?'

Before the Bishop could answer Lawrence caught his father's hand.

'Father! There is no need to cast lots! Let me be the one! I shall never be happy away from Glendalough.'

So when The O'Toole rode away, the three boys who had ridden with him went back to Castle Dermot, and Lawrence stayed in the care of the Bishop.

## MacMurrough and the Normans

Now Lawrence's home was in Glendalough and he was happy there. He studied, helped to receive guests, taught younger students, travelled, but always returned. As soon as he was old enough he was ordained a priest and went out preaching. The people in the valley knew him well, and even the outlaws in the hills had a friendship for this young man who climbed steep rocks like a goat and walked up to their camp fires without a sign of fear.

Lawrence was only twenty-five when he was made Abbot. The next day, when he went out into the misty morning, he saw a crowd of people sitting and lying on the ground outside the gate.

He looked at them through the bars. They were thin and wretched. All gazed at him appealingly, but not one spoke.

'What ails you, my children?' he asked.

An old man tottered to the gate.

'We are starving! Our crops have failed, our beasts

have perished. We haven't a crust of bread or a drop of milk for the children. Have pity on us!'

Lawrence unbarred the gate and flung both sides wide open.

'Come in!' he said. 'The guest hall is prepared. You shall not be kept waiting.'

They swarmed about the young Abbot as he led the way into the big hall. The monks came running and, before the wind had blown away the mist, great bowls of hot porridge were placed down the centre of the tables. All the benches in the monastery were brought down for the people. But there were so many that most of them had to sit on the floor.

As the bowls were emptied Lawrence saw more people crowding up the path to the gate. These came from the far side of the mountains, yet they told the same story – the crops had failed, their cattle had perished.

' 'Twas the late frosts!' one man told Lawrence.

'Not at all!' shouted several together. ' 'Twas the twenty-one days' drought!'

The Abbot heard how the seed shrivelled in the ground, the grass was brown and the earth like hot powder.

'It's a famine,' the oldest of the monks told him. 'There hasn't been one like it for years! How shall we feed them all? What shall we do when all our provisions are gone?'

'When the time comes we shall learn!' replied Lawrence.

Whole villages came trooping into the courtyard until it was like a tinkers' encampment. Outside, on every level patch of ground, some family sat down, and there they all waited for the young Abbot to feed them.

'Take what money we have,' said Lawrence to the monk who had charge of the stores, when the last bit of food in the monastery was eaten. 'Buy food! The people must be fed!'

All the money in the monastery was spent. Lawrence exchanged manuscripts and anything of value he could find for more food. He sent to his family, the O'Tooles, for help, and to everyone he knew. Cartloads of food came trundling over the causeway and, by the time of the next harvest, the young Abbot could boast that he had not refused food to one of the people who had asked for it.

He was made Archbishop of Dublin and had to leave Glendalough. He had a grand house in Dublin, where his biggest table was made to seat thirty poor people who had dinner there every day.

He went back to his real home as often as he could. He had a cell cut out of the rock above the upper lake where he could see the sunrise over the mountains and watch fish leaping in the dark pool below.

All this time Dermot MacMurrough had been raiding and fighting with the chiefs of Leinster and Munster. With the help of the High King Roderic, O'Rourke of Breffni led an army against MacMurrough. Dermot was hated by his own people for his cruelty, and now they deserted him. He burned his castle at Ferns and fled to England.

The princes of Leinster and Munster pronounced a sentence of banishment against him and appointed his cousin, MacMurrough na Gael, or Murrough of the Irish, in his place. From this time Dermot MacMurrough was called Dermott na Gall, or Dermot of the Strangers.

Once he reached England, MacMurrough went in search of Henry the Second, the most powerful king in Europe. Henry was in France, fighting his own barons, but was very willing to help in an attack upon Ireland. He gave MacMurrough a letter authorizing him to organize an expedition against the Irish princes.

For a while MacMurrough could get no one to go back with him until he met with Richard de Clare, Earl of Pembroke, called Strongbow, because of his great skill in archery. With him were two Anglo-Norman knights, Maurice Fitzgerald and Robert Fitzstephen. They agreed to help MacMurrough invade Ireland if he would grant them large estates.

This was the beginning of the Norman invasion of Ireland. Saint Lawrence was at Glendalough when news came that Dermot MacMurrough had returned and was hiding at Ferns, near his own castle. Soon after, the Archbishop heard that a party of Anglo-Normans had landed at Bannow Bay in County Wexford, and that MacMurrough was joining them with five hundred men.

The invaders attacked the city of Wexford, but the townspeople fought all night and beat off the attack. The next day, when MacMurrough and his allies were preparing an assault, the people offered to surrender and Dermot entered the city.

After capturing Wexford, MacMurrough led his party back to Ferns, where they rebuilt the burnt-out building, gathered a large army together and prepared for attack.

Roderic O'Connor, High King of Ireland, was a pleasant, easy-going man, quite unfit to rule the country in such troubled times. While MacMurrough and the Normans were strengthening themselves the High King was celebrating the Tailteann Games at Tara.

So many armed men were gathered there that their tents covered a space of six and a half miles. Had Brian Boru been alive, had Lawrence O'Toole been king, the Norman invasion would have ended in a week.

MacMurrough, realizing that the King was not prepared to attack him, marched with an army of 3,000, as well as the Normans, into Ossory, territory of an old enemy. Here he was successful, and at last the High King was roused to the danger.

He marched to Ferns with an army quite large enough to crush MacMurrough. Instead of fighting, King Roderic offered terms first to Fitzstephen and then to Dermot MacMurrough.

Fugitives from Ossory brought news of what was happening in the south to the Archbishop in Dublin. While Lawrence O'Toole was expecting to hear of MacMurrough's surrender, Roderic had acknowledged Dermot as King of Leinster on condition that he sent away his foreign allies.

Roderic marched away with his army, taking MacMurrough's son with him as hostage. All this time letters were being sent to Strongbow. Each letter promised him more and more if he would come to MacMurrough's help. He was offered large grants of land and MacMurrough agreed that if Strongbow would only hasten, his daughter Eva would marry him and he would succeed MacMurrough as King of Leinster.

The Normans were adventurers, daring and greedy, but such good fighters MacMurrough thought himself lucky to have them for allies. The moment he learned that Strongbow had landed, he set out to meet the Norman, and together they marched against Waterford.

### Lawrence Tries to Make Peace

Roderic, with his army, waited for the enemy at Clondalkin, a village south of Dublin. While he encamped there,

Dermot led his allies through the Wicklow mountains and marched to Dublin by the coast.

Dublin was a walled city, but the citizens were terrified by the mail-clad knights and men-at-arms, as well as by the stories that were being told of their fierceness and cruelty.

Lawrence O'Toole's house was beseiged by people imploring him to save them and to make a treaty with the Anglo-Normans.

The Archbishop went out to the foreigners' camp. While he appealed to them, two of the Norman knights with their followers made a breach in the walls of the city and entered the streets. They burned houses and killed the unarmed people.

The noise and tumult reached the camp and so Lawrence heard of the massacre.

He hurried back to Dublin and succeeded in stopping the slaughter. Hourly he expected the Irish army to appear and save the city. But Roderic, one of the weakest kings Ireland ever had, marched his men away from Dublin, and Milo de Cogan, a Norman knight, became its governor.

MacMurrough and the Normans went through the country burning churches, castles, and even the cabins.

It seemed as if nothing could stop MacMurrough when, suddenly, he died at Ferns. Strongbow proclaimed himself King of Leinster, but Henry of England, who wanted Ireland for himself, ordered him to return.

'This is our chance to rid ourselves of these Normans!' declared Lawrence O'Toole.

He travelled through Ireland, urging the princes to unite and attack the invaders before reinforcements could come from England. In this the Archbishop was so successful that even Roderic was convinced success was possible. He agreed to lead the Irish army in an attempt to overwhelm the Normans.

Strongbow ignored Henry the Second's command and, instead of going back to England, hastened to Dublin and prepared to defend himself against the united Irish.

The High King encamped at Castleknock, a village at the western end of what is now the Phoenix Park. Lawrence O'Toole was also at the camp and, every hour, armed men were hurrying in to join the battle.

Messengers brought Strongbow the news of what was happening and he realized that he could not hold out. He sent to the Archbishop, offering to hold Leinster as a vassal of King Roderic. The Irish refused his offer and declared that he must surrender the cities of Dublin, Waterford and Wexford and depart from Ireland.

Strongbow had decided to agree to these terms when Donal O'Kavanagh, son of Dermot MacMurrough, entered Dublin in disguise. He came from Fitzstephen, who was besieged in the castle of Ferrycarrig, near Wexford, and who implored Strongbow to send him help or he must surrender.

Strongbow was in despair. The city was surrounded, while a fleet blockaded the harbour. It was impossible to obtain provisions, and the Irish chiefs, satisfied that the Normans' surrender was sure, contented themselves with the blockade and did not make any assault on the city.

Maurice Fitzgerald suggested that a small band of the Normans should make a sortie and attempt to force a way out. It was a summer afternoon. King Roderic and his friends were bathing in the Liffey. The Normans, well-armed, brilliant fighters, found the Irish army quite unprepared for them. Many were killed at once and the rest fled in panic, while the High King barely escaped.

The Normans were amazed at their success. They

raided the Irish camp and marched back to Dublin loaded with arms, clothes and provisions.

Leaving Milo de Cogan in charge of the city, Strongbow set off south to save Robert Fitzstephen. When the Wexford men heard of his approach they had already captured Ferrycarrig Castle, and Fitzstephen and his men were in their hands.

They retreated with the prisoners to the island of Begerin and sent word to Strongbow that, if he attacked, they would cut off the heads of his friends. So the Normans retreated to Waterford.

Roderic now decided to make a treaty with Henry the Second and asked Lawrence O'Toole to cross to England and see the King. The Archbishop set off at once. Henry heard of his coming, refused to see him and departed for Normandy.

He expected Lawrence to return to Ireland. The Archbishop followed him. Unfortunately for Ireland, Lawrence O'Toole was worn out with hard work and worry. He fell ill at the monastery of Eu in Normandy. When he was asked by the monks to make his will he smiled.

'Thanks be to God,' he told them, 'I have not one penny in the world to dispose of,' and died happily.

He was the last of the Irish saints as Roderic was the last King.

# THERE WERE OTHER SAINTS

Saint Ciaran, the carpenter's son,
Who built great Clonmacnoise;
Saint Ita, who cared for so many saints,
The mother of them all;
Dymphna, the Lily of Erin,
Who fled from a cruel king;
Mobhi, the great, of Glasnevin
And Finbarr, saint of the south,
Who lived up at lone Gougane Barra,
That wild and desolate lake.

There was Ultan, who pitied lost children;
Columbanus, who went far away
Among savage men and wild beasts.
Knowing no fear, he tamed them all;
Then old, but never weary, he went to Bobbio,
Cut down the fir trees, climbed the Appenines.

Colman was a happy saint.
He had no clock,
But a crowing cock,
No house, but a friendly mouse;
And, just before his cell
Where the water fell,
Wide and clear and cool,
In a rock-bound pool,
Swam his flock of ducks,
When the light was gone
The day's work done,
On tiny rainbow wings

## KNIGHTS OF GOD

Fluttered a fly
Down to the holy book
Where Colman read
And, settling on the page,
Kept there his place.

So many names – they crowd on every page
Of Ireland's story in that Golden Age.

# LIST OF BOOKS

❧

For details concerning the lives of the Irish saints I found the following books useful: –

*Beasts and Saints.* By Helen Waddell.
*St Brigid of Ireland.* By Alice Curtayne.
*St Brendan: the Voyager and his Mystic Quest.* By James Wylkie.
*St Patrick.* By Rt Rev M. J. O'Farrell, Bishop of Trenton.
*Saint Patrick.* By Hugh De Blacam.
*I Follow St Patrick.* By Oliver St John Gogarty.
*Lives of Irish Saints.* By Charles Plummer, M.A.
*St Patrick: The Travelling Man.* By W. M. Letts.
*Ireland and the Early Church.* By J. M. Flood.
*Irish Saints in Italy.* By Fra Anselmo M. Tommasini, O.F.M.
*Bedside Book of Irish Saints.* By Rev Aloysius Roche.
*Lives of the Saints.* By Alban Butler.
*Ireland's Ancient Schools and Scholars.* By Rev John Healy, D.D., LL.D.
*Myths and Legends of the Celtic Race.* By T. W. Rolleston.
*Legends of Saints and Sinners.* By Douglas Hyde.
*A Book of Saints and Wonders.* By Lady Gregory.
*Historic Struggles for the Faith.* By John Gabriel Rowe.
*The Islands of Ireland.* By Thomas H. Mason.
*The Transition from Roman Britain to Christian England.* By Gilbert Sheldon.
*Catholic Encyclopedia.*
*Smith's Dictionary of Names.*

If you have enjoyed this book and would like to know about others which we publish, why not join the Puffin Club? You will receive the club magazine, *Puffin Post*, four times a year and a smart badge and membership book. You will also be able to enter all the competitions. Write for an application form to:

*The Puffin Club Secretary*
*Penguin Books Limited*
*Bath Road,*
*Harmondsworth*
*Middlesex*